Quiet Women Never Changed History Be Strong, Stand Up and Stand Out

Quiet Women Never Changed History Be Strong, Stand Up and Stand Out

LET'S GO KICK SOME GLASS!

Pattie S. Grimm

ISBN-13: 9780692742419
ISBN-10: 0692742417
Library of Congress Control Number: 2016912099
Pattie Grimm, Laguna Niguel, CA

TABLE OF CONTENTS

Acknowledgments · vii

Introduction · ix

Chapter 1   The Glass Ceiling Is Cracking—Now,
             Let's Kick Some Glass! · 1

Chapter 2   I Never Thought It Would Happen to Me · · · · · · · · · · · 5

Chapter 3   My Three-Year Research Study Findings · · · · · · · · · · 10

Chapter 4   So, What Is a Leader? · 19

Chapter 5   Leaders in Your Life · 24

Section 1 – My Leadership Journey

Chapter 6   My Story—The Early Days · · · · · · · · · · · · · · · · · · 29

Section 2 – Be Strong

Chapter 7   Deb's Story—Breaking through at West Point · · · · · · · 51

Chapter 8   Self-Knowledge and Self-Mastery—Keys to
             Your Success as a Leader · · · · · · · · · · · · · · · · · · 54

Chapter 9   Leveraging Your Strengths and Being
             the Best Leader You Can Be · · · · · · · · · · · · · · · · · · 59

Chapter 10   Birds of a Feather Flock Together—Self-Awareness · · · · 62

Chapter 11   Leverage Your Strengths and Maintain Your Peak
             Performance · 67

Chapter 12   Personal Styles and Leadership · · · · · · · · · · · · · · · · · 70
Chapter 13   Change Is Hard and Takes Practice, Patience, and
              Persistence · 73

Section 3 – Stand Up

Chapter 14   Cathy's Story · 81
Chapter 15   Being a Great Leader and Coach · · · · · · · · · · · · · · · · 86
Chapter 16   Develop Your Personal and
              Professional Vision—You Inc. · · · · · · · · · · · · · · · · · · 88

Section 4 – Stand Out

Chapter 17   Building Your Self-Confidence · · · · · · · · · · · · · · · · 103
Chapter 18   What's Wrong with Being Confident? · · · · · · · · · · · 105
Chapter 19   Practice Self-Care and Self-Love · · · · · · · · · · · · · · 109
Chapter 20   The Power of Positive Affirmations · · · · · · · · · · · · 113
Chapter 21   Forgive and Forget and Let It Go · · · · · · · · · · · · · · 122
Chapter 22   Being the Best Leader You Can Be · · · · · · · · · · · · · 128
Chapter 23   The Power of Feedback · 133
Chapter 24   The Myth of Doing It All · · · · · · · · · · · · · · · · · · · 140

Section 5 – Summary and Final Action Plan

Chapter 25   Eva's Story · 145
Chapter 26   Be Strong, Stand Up, and Stand Out by Helping
              Other Women Succeed · 148
Chapter 27   My Personal Seven Things Every Woman
              Should Do · 156

              About the Author · 161

ACKNOWLEDGMENTS

*The time is long overdue to encourage more
women to dream the possible dream!*
—SHERYL SANDBERG, AUTHOR OF *LEAN IN*

I want to thank my book-review team for reading the first draft of my book and providing helpful feedback on how to improve it and increase its impact. Each of these women is a good friend and has been a teammate at some point in my career. Each is a passionate, strong, and successful leader in her own area of expertise.

My review team consisted of the following women:

Yvonne Erickson
Cynthia Sward
Laura Steward

I want to thank my awesome husband, Ross, who has stood by me through the good times, the bad times, and the ugly times. I want to thank my kids, Ross III and Elke, for being great children and now amazing adults. I want to thank my adorable pug, Roxie, for being an endless source of joy, laughter, and good times.

A special thanks to my parents in heaven, because I know they are up there, looking down on me and helping me today, even though they are gone from this earth. I am convinced they are up in heaven, kicking up their heels, square dancing in matching outfits. When I was a teenager, the fact my parents square danced and wore matching outfits was a great source of embarrassment. Now, I find it cute and touching.

I also want to thank my brother, Mike, and my baby sister, Christine, for being a part of my life. Mike and I grew up together, and our family moved a lot. We learned to stick together and adapt to a new home or change easily. My sister, Christine, was born when I was fifteen years old. She brought a new joy and life to our family. Things like Christmas, Easter, and other holidays became special again when Christine came into our lives.

I want to thank the many leaders in my life for helping me become the person I am today. I want to thank the good managers and leaders for being role models and helping me learn how to be a better leader. I want to thank the "bad" or negative leaders in my life for helping me learn how to never be the kind of manager they were.

Finally, I want to acknowledge and thank every person I interviewed or who responded to my survey. Your thoughts, stories, and suggestions are a core part of this book. You expanded my thinking and point of view and motivated me to finally finish the book.

INTRODUCTION

This Book Is for You

Sometimes you learn more from your losses than your wins!
—PAT SUMMIT, UNIVERSITY OF TENNESSEE
WOMEN'S BASKETBALL COACH

Please read this introduction!
I finished this book on July 4, 2016, just before heading to a Fourth of July party at a friend's house with a great view of the ocean and the fireworks. I wrote this book as part of my passion to help empower women of all ages to be the best leader or person they can be; in any endeavor they choose.

I also wrote this book to help other women learn from my successes and challenges as well as from those of the women I interviewed for this book. I started this book project three years ago after I experienced what I call "the fall." I went from being a very successful woman at the top of the corporate mountain to being at the bottom of the mountain in a depression-like state. I managed to pull myself up and out of this low state. I hope this book will help other women either avoid the fall or recognize they are falling sooner so they can recover faster than I did.

The title of this book comes from a quote by Madam Marie Curie: "Quiet women never change history." Madam Curie was a female doctor and scientist at a time when there were very few women in the field of medicine. She changed the world and made it a better place, even though she eventually died from the very disease she was trying to cure.

I use this quote because I find it to be true. The title does not mean you need to be a loud, aggressive, or bossy leader; in fact, it means the exact opposite. The title means women need to be strong, stand up, and stand out as passionate and effective leaders in any field they choose and in their own style.

The best practices and recommended practical exercises come from my personal experience as a female leader in several very male-dominated fields. In addition, I conducted hundreds of personal interviews and received over 1,850 responses from men and women on my leadership questionnaire. I'll share these best practices throughout the book.

This book is a gift of my love and deep passion for empowering strong and successful female leaders of all ages. This book is intended to help you by providing insights and practical exercises to help you excel in any endeavor you choose.

If you're a young girl or woman just starting in your career, this book is for you. If you're a woman in her mid-twenties or mid-thirties and struggling to balance your career and your family, this book is for you. If you're a woman who is a stay-at-home mom who volunteers at your kids' school, this book is for you.

If you are a father with a daughter in your life, this book is for you and your daughter. If you are a brother or uncle with young women you care about, this book is for you.

I've read literally hundreds of self-help books, leadership books, and books for women leaders. Most leadership books I've read talk a lot about *what* you need to do to be a great and effective leader. Most self-help books tell you *how* to improve your personal life. In my book, I am attempting to do both. Based on my own experience and the combined experiences of the people who participated in my leadership survey, I provide the *what* and the *how* of putting some of these practices to work in your life.

One thing this book is not—it is not about male or male-leader bashing. There are many wonderful and very successful male leaders in the world. I've been fortunate to work for or work with a lot of great male leaders who inspired me and helped me be a better leader and person. This book is written to help more women become the leaders they can be.

How This Book Is Organized

This book is a little different since most books in this area focus either on the personal side or on the leadership side of life. This book combines a little of both with practical exercises to apply in your life.

The book is organized into six sections. Each section starts with a small portion of a song, written or performed by a popular female artist, that I found very inspiring and that has helped me throughout my career and life.

Each section contains a series of shorter chapters and starts with a story about me or one of the women who participated in my research, followed by a series of suggested personal or leadership success strategies and exercises.

The final portion of each chapter or section has a "Personal Leadership Application Exercise" to help you put together an action plan to empower you, to give you a greater sense of accomplishment, and to help you become the best person you can be and truly reach your full potential.

I don't expect everyone who reads this book to put all these ideas to work. You need to pick the ones that work for you. Try them on, and adjust them to your style. Pick a few to work on first, and then add others as you see the need.

The application exercises start with looking at the personal or internal side of being a strong and successful female leader. In my humble opinion, you need to start and build from the inside out before you can work on the business side of leadership. Possibly one of the reasons some of the recent research shows that female leaders are better than male leaders in some areas is that women tend to have more empathy and intuition. Women tend to lead from inside out. Men tend to lead from the outside first.

These exercises are intended to guide you through each area and help you become the kind of leader you want to be. After all, this book is for you and the people you lead.

Throughout the book, I share best practices in the form of stories, real-life examples, and practical strategies that you can put into action to become a strong and successful leader at any age and regardless of your chosen endeavor or life choice.

My goal is to write a book to help women of all ages become the best leaders they can be. One of my goals is to get my readers to stretch their minds and be open to learning or trying a few new things. We all learn when we read, hear, or see something new and different; compare this new information with what we already know; and then decide whether or not to apply this new information.

Here is a personal example of my learning. I was participating in a Six Sigma data-driven training session many years ago. Six Sigma training is all about data and facts, and you'll find out later that details and facts are not my strengths.

I was completely lost at one point when we were calculating standard deviation without the aid of a smart calculator that did it automatically. To be honest, I felt like the dumbest person in the room. At break, I went up to the instructor and told him I was lost.

He responded, "Great...that means you're learning." Then he reminded me that the famous Dr. W. Edwards Deming, who was one of the founding fathers and gurus of things like Six Sigma, said, "If you're struggling, you are learning. If something comes easy to you, you already know it and no learning is occurring!"

Turning Moments into Momentum

Your life can change in a moment. You meet someone new and develop a long-term friendship. You break up with a long-term friend or boyfriend and find someone better. You might have worked your life to get to a certain place, and then in one moment, something happens to make it come true.

For me one, of the moments, as I mentioned earlier, was the inspiration to finish this book. I'd been told I should write a book on leadership for many years. I resisted writing a leadership book because there were hundreds of great leadership books out there by PhDs and people much smarter than I am.

The first moment I got inspired to write a book for women leaders in this case was when I left Microsoft after fifteen years and restarted my consulting company. I had a moment and let it pass because I let my own lack of self-confidence and my doubt stop me from writing after about a year.

The second moment, which I'll talk about later in the book, happened on Easter Sunday in church. This time, I took that simple moment and moved it from *one moment into momentum.* I was compelled to write and wrote something every day for two and a half months.

I would wake up in the middle of the night and feel compelled to write down the thoughts that were spinning in my head. I found signs, quotes, and inspiration around every corner. My confidence came back, and my business started to flourish.

My question to you as you read this book is: What are the moments in your life, and how can you turn these moments into momentum to propel you forward in a new positive direction?

Little girls with dreams become women with vision.
(Unknown)

CHAPTER 1

THE GLASS CEILING IS CRACKING—NOW, LET'S KICK SOME GLASS!

*Never doubt that a small group of people can change
the world; indeed, it is the only thing that ever has!*
—MARGARET MEAD, AMERICAN ANTHROPOLOGIST

History was made in June 2016 when Hillary Rodham Clinton was announced as the first woman to win a major party nomination to be president of the United States. In her speech in New York on this historic day, Hilary said, "This is a grand day in history when any little girl can be anything she wants to be, even president of the United States of America!"

Another history-making event happened on June 8, 2016, when Serena Williams, the great tennis pro, became the highest-paid athlete in the world. This was a glass-breaking event and a very positive sign to come for all of us. We now need for every woman to be paid the same as her male counterpart doing the same job. We need more women sitting at the top of business organizations and charitable organizations.

A third major event occurred in June 2016 as I was writing this book; we lost a legend in the sports world and a legendary female leader. Pat Summit, the former women's basketball coach from the University of Tennessee, died of dementia at the age of sixty-four. The headlines in the newspaper the morning after Pat died read, "A TRUE TRAILBLAZER."

Pat's leadership goes far beyond her amazing record as the coach of the University of Tennessee Volunteers women's basketball team. Pat coached the women's basketball team from 1974 to 2012 when she retired because of her illness. She was offered the job to coach the men's team, and she refused the offer because she wanted to work with the women's team and help them become the best they could be. This might seem like a small thing, but in the college-sports world, the ceiling that blocks women from becoming a men's coach is described as the "concrete ceiling," not the "glass ceiling."

Yes, Pat had an amazing record as a coach, but it is what she did off the court that really mattered. She overcame unbelievable obstacles during her career, including the fact that in the early days, the women's team was forced to sleep on the floor in the gym of the opposing team when they traveled to games because of a lack of funding for the women's program. The men's teams had plenty of money, so they stayed in a hotel close to their game.

Many of the men's college programs are given sanctions or penalties for illegal recruiting, paying college players to play or other such activities. Pat's women's team had zero sanctions in thirty-eight years. Pat's winning record was 1,098 wins to 208 loses. She was NCAA Coach of the Year seven times, more times than any male coach. Pat won more championship and conference titles than any male coach and was awarded the Presidential Medal of Freedom in 2012.

Yes, Pat's on-the-court accomplishments were incredible, but they pale in comparison to her off-the-court accomplishments. You see, Pat had a 100 percent graduation rate, meaning all of her players over the course of thirty-eight years graduated from college. There is not a male coach on the planet whose record can compare to hers. Roughly calculated, Pat coached over one thousand young women to become great players and great leaders in business, in their community, and in the world as a whole.

We all stand on the shoulders of giants, and it is our job to continue this momentum going forward. Women like Pat, Susan B. Anthony, Helen Gurley Brown, and Sally Helgesen started this revolution. It is now our job to build on their successes and take it to the next level.

We have great current role models in women like Sheryl Sandberg, who started the Lean-In movement, and Arianna Huffington, who not only runs the *Huffington Post* but wrote a great book called *Thrive*. We have women like Irene Rosenfeld, chairman and CEO of Kraft Foods; Indra Nooyi, chairman and CEO of PepsiCo; and Ursula M. Burns, chairman and CEO of Xerox as role models. We also have a lot of women like those I interviewed who are succeeding as leaders at their own levels as a team leaders, troop leaders, or managers.

We have Queen Elizabeth II, who is one of the longest-reigning monarchs, and other women like Chancellor Angela Merkel of Germany and Hillary Rodham Clinton, currently running to be the first female president of the United States, in the political world leading the change.

I love this quote from Margaret Thatcher:

"If you want anything said, ask a man. If you want something done, ask a woman."

Later in this book, I'll talk about the fact we've come a long way as women of the world since the early days but we still have a long way to go. I hope that by writing this book, I can in some way help other women of the world become the best people they can be and help them reach their full potential at any age and in any endeavor they choose.

The other side of the coin for the girls and women of the world is dealing with the internal barriers we place upon ourselves. Limiting self-beliefs and negative self-talk sometimes hold us back as much as, if not more than, the external barriers in the world.

While we all need to continue to push for things like equal pay for equal work, we need to face our inner thoughts, beliefs, and actions because they are 100 percent in our control. We may or may not be able to change someone's opinion of us, but we can change, adjust, modify, and improve our own opinions of ourselves.

This book is intended to help more little girls, young women, and mature women dream a little bigger and more often, shine a little brighter, and change their world.

CHAPTER 2

I Never Thought It Would Happen to Me

My Story—The Short Version

Let me start with my story and what drove me or motivated me to write this book in the first place. I'll go into more detail about my story later in the book.

To most people, I grew up a middle child in a blessed and typical middle-class family. I was blessed because I had a mom, dad, older brother, and younger sister who loved me. I was blessed because I had a lot of amazing friends and coworkers in my personal and professional life. I was blessed because I have more positive memories of my life than negative ones. I had a lot of ups and downs but probably more ups than downs.

So, I never thought it would happen to me, but it did. I had a life filled with loving and caring people, but after all these amazing experiences, I found myself at the bottom of the barrel with extreme chronic fatigue, exhausted, and on the verge of depression.

How had I let myself get to this state where I was literally dragging myself out of bed and trying to put on my happy face? How had I become the person who struggled to have a conversation with people when I used to be the person who loved to entertain and be the life of the party?

How had I allowed other people's image of me and my personal worth to become more important than my own? How had I allowed my mind, self-esteem, and self-worth to be controlled by someone other than myself?

This book is about my highs, my fall, my stumble, and my recovery.

Always remember life is a journey and not a destination. Half of the fun in life is learning, making mistakes, and growing. Be a lifelong learner by attending classes, reading books, and learning from every experience because that is where the fun and growth begins.

Think like a queen. A queen is not afraid to fail.
Failure is another steppingstone to greatness.
—OPRAH WINFREY

We've Come a Long Way Baby, and We Have a Long Way to Go

Many times when I give my speeches, training classes, and webinars to young women in their twenties and thirties, I have one or two of these young women come up and tell me that they are not experiencing the same kind of challenges I am describing. I understand where they are coming from since we all stand on the shoulders of giants and powerful women who came before us. I sincerely hope these young women are right.

Today, we have women like Sheryl Sandberg, who wrote *Lean In*; Arianna Huffington, who wrote *Thrive*; and my good friend Laura Steward Atchison, who wrote, *What Would a Wise Woman Do*. We stand on the shoulders of the giants and glass-ceiling breakers who came before us.

I highly recommend you buy all three of these books because they are based on valuable research and provide a lot of examples on how to be a strong female leader.

Sheryl provides valuable insights from her experiences at Google and Facebook on how we need to lean in together and help other women achieve success. She discusses her research on how women don't negotiate, especially for things like salary like men. She provides an example of how she doubted how much she was worth when she was negotiating with Mark Zuckerberg to join Facebook.

Arianna tells her story of how she woke up one day with blood running down her face. She was so exhausted from working too many long days without a break that she fell asleep at her desk. She talks about the importance of sleep, taking time to recover, and taking care of yourself.

Arianna recently announced she is retiring from being the CEO of the *Huffington Post* to focus on her cause and help people improve their productivity.

Laura's book demonstrates the power of using questions to provide insights into your life. Her approach to asking insightful questions when faced with a job or life challenge helped me when I was deciding whether to stay or leave Microsoft after a great fifteen-year career.

Here are a few facts that indicate we as women leaders still have a long way to go. In the seventies, women made fifty-nine cents on the dollar as compared to men. Today we earn seventy-one cents. Women's pay equality has only improved 1 percent in the last few years. If we continue at this pace of change, we won't reach pay equality for over one hundred years. Marlo Thomas said it best: "Even a loaf of bread or gallon of milk has increased more than our pay!"

There are still too few women at top-level executive positions in major companies and boards. Both external and internal barriers exist to women being seen as equal to or better than men.

In 2015, McKinsey & Company partnered with the Lean In Organization and conducted an extensive research study called *Women in the Workplace 2015*. It was a comprehensive study of the state of women in corporate America.

They reported that women are still underrepresented. Corporate America's not on a fast-track path to gender equality. Here is a quote from the report:

> our analysis tells the complex story, women face greater barriers to advancement and a steeper path to senior leadership. Female leadership is imperative for organizations that want to perform at a higher level. Yet, based on the progress the last three years, it will take twenty-five years to reach gender parity at the senior VP level and more than a hundred years to reach the C-suite.

Here are some additional facts from the report:

- Women are underrepresented at every level—45 percent of the entry-level managers are women, 32 percent at senior management, and only 17 percent at the C-suite level, up only 1 percent from 2012.

- The report stated women are not leaving organizations at a higher level than men.
- CEOs are usually promoted from line roles more than staff roles. Line roles have profit-and-loss responsibility, and a high percentage of C-suite executives are in line roles.
- Women face great challenges getting to the C-suite because most women in senior vice president and lower-level positions are in staff roles like human resources, information technology (IT), and operations.
- Women with children are 15 percent more interested in being a top executive than women without children.
- Finally, only 28 percent of senior-level women are happy with their careers, as compared to 40 percent of the men.

In addition to the external barriers listed above, many of the internal barriers women like me experienced have not gotten better or gone away. These internal barriers include our own self-doubt. We ask ourselves, "Am I really worth this amount of money, or do I have the skills to do the next level job?"

Here is an interesting fact: men get promoted based on potential, and women get promoted based on performance, meaning women have to prove to their managers that they are ready for a promotion while men are promoted if they *might* have the potential to grow into the position.

Sheryl Sandberg makes an interesting point about potential versus performance. She provides the example of a great job being posted for a higher-level management position. She says a man looks at the job posting, which requires ten specific skills or experiences. Even if the man only has five of the required skills or experiences, he'll apply for the job.

A woman, however, sees the same job posting and requirements. She has nine of the required skills and experiences, and she will not apply more often than not. She'll think, I need more experience, or I'll go back to school to fill in the gaps.

I credit my mom and dad for the many blessings in my life and helping me to be successful. They instilled in me a sense of confidence and belief in my potential. I was taught to take pride in my performance.

I grew up in a sports family, which I really believe helped me early in my career in banking. Sports helped me fit in in the late 1980s when there were few women in leadership positions in banks. I was a vice president of a major California bank at the age of twenty-seven. Trust me, you don't need to be a sports fan or athlete to succeed, but it certainly helped me throughout my career.

My dad also taught me to appreciate cars. I could not get my license until I could learn to drive his truck with a three on the column stick shift. I also had to learn how to change a tire and the spark plugs. My dad wanted me to be self-sufficient.

My mom and dad always told me I could do or be anything I wanted to be. They told me I was just as smart as any boy or man. Of course, my mom's idea of the perfect career for me was to be a flight attendant and my dad's idea was to be an engineer like him.

People who know me laugh at these two possible career choices. They laugh at the idea of me being a flight attendant because they know the minute a passenger got unruly, I would dump a cup of hot coffee on his or her lap. I would make a terrible engineer even though I was good at math because I am not a detail-oriented person and would have trouble following strict guidelines.

Let's start with my research as a basis for the book and the recommendations in the book.

CHAPTER 3

My Three-Year Research Study Findings

I don't want to bore people with a lot of research, facts, and figures, but I do want to share some of the insights I gained from the three years of research and the interviews behind this book. The best part of the interview process was hearing and reading the personal stories of women who overcame obstacles to become successful and effective leaders.

I used a standard interview protocol to allow for a consistent assimilation of the data. The main questions I asked were as follows:

1. What are the characteristics or behaviors of a strong and effective female leader?
2. Is there a difference between a strong female and a strong male leader? If yes, what are the differences? If no, why not?
3. What are the biggest barriers to women truly breaking through the glass ceiling and making it to the executive level, commonly referred to as the C-suite (CEO, CFO, CMO, and so on)?
4. Are these barriers more internal or external? Why?
5. What best practices have you used or seen great female leaders put into action to succeed?

My Research Findings

When I started my journey to write this book, I was so excited and passionate about this project. I looked forward to every interview as a chance to learn something and connect with some great people. I am pleasantly surprised that over 250 people I asked for an hour of their time to do a personal interview responded with a yes. In fact, at the completion of every interview, people would give me the names of two to three other people to interview as well.

Each interview far exceeded my expectations, and I felt incredibly motivated about every interview. My first question in the interviews and on the online survey was "What are the characteristics of a strong and effective female leader?"

The following graph shows the responses to this question.

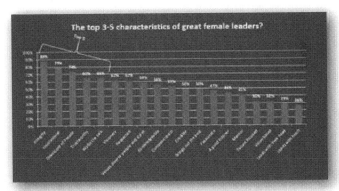

The top ten characteristics were not that different from the list of characteristics of a great male leader or a leader in general. However, the order or ranking the of characteristics appear in is slightly different. Most lists of top male leaders start with *visionary, strategic, knowledgeable, and respected,* followed by *inspirational, developer of people,* and so on. The top characteristics of female leaders are more internal—having *integrity* and being *inspirational* and *developers of people.*

Top Ten Women Leader Characteristics	Top Ten General Leader Characteristics
Integrity	Results oriented
Inspirational	Strategic thinker
Developer of people	Decision maker
Trustworthy	Visionary
Walk the talk	Works well with others
Visionary	Deals with conflict

Respected	Customer focused
Values diverse styles and people	Good listener
Knowledgeable	Good communicator
Compassionate	Trustworthy

The second question resulted in a very interesting and enlightening discussion in every interview. "Is there a difference between a great female leader and a great male leader?"

The following table shows some of the common differences mentioned during the interviews and the responses to the online survey.

Women	Men
see around the corners	good listeners
gather consensus, then decide	quick decision makers
bring out the best in the team	good team builders
strategic thinkers—people first	strategic thinkers—facts first
trustworthy and walks the talk	creditable

One of the most interesting responses was from one female leader I interviewed who said, "Women see around the corners." She said men can be insightful, empathic, and compassionate, but women tend to do it more naturally or by instinct. For example, a team is in a meeting and the discussion is getting quite heated. People are starting to raise their voices. The male leader will simply continue on in the meeting and not notice that one or more of the team members seems uncomfortable with the way the conversation is going.

The female leader, however, will notice the one (or more) team member who seems uncomfortable or disengaged and try to draw that person into the meeting by asking a question. The woman is more likely to talk to the person after the meeting and ask if he or she is all right than the male leader.

When it comes to decision making, men tend to make faster or quicker decisions and gather consensus or feedback on the decision later. Women tend to gather consensus or feedback and then make the decision. Neither one is right or wrong.

Men tend to be strategic thinkers, based on facts more than people. Woman leaders tend to be strategic thinkers based on people and then the facts. Again, neither is right nor wrong.

The fact is women and men are *hardwired* differently. Scientists have found men's and women's brain patterns are different. The scientists studied men's and women's responses using an MRI machine. Men's brain waves go left and right or front and back in a predictable pattern. Women's brain patterns moved in a far more random pattern and jumped from left to front and from back to right, which might be why women are better at multitasking than men.[1]

The old book *Men Are from Mars and Women Are from Venus* is true. We are simply hardwired differently. Some of recent research indicates that women are in some cases better leaders than men, especially with the millennials, which I discuss later in the book.

---

1 There is a very funny video about the differences between men's and women's brains by Mark Ungor on YouTube at https://www.bing.com/videos/search?q=U+tube+-+difference+betwen+men+and+women%3bs+brains&&view=detail&mid=DE6766F84A16C959B996DE6766F84A16C959B996&rvsmid=FA2F0307536EBD8949EDFA2F0307536EBD8949ED&fsscr=0&FORM=VDQVAP. In a very funny way, he supports the scientific research, which was conducted by measuring the brain wave patterns of men's and women's brains.

The next question in the interviews and on the online survey was "What are the biggest barriers to women's success as leaders, and are the barriers more internal or external?"

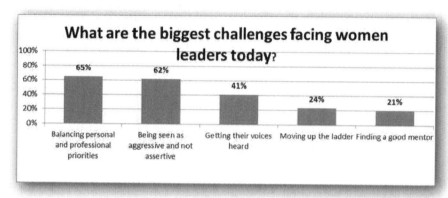

The response on whether the barriers facing women today were internal or external was a closer split with 59 percent external and 41 percent internal. Internal barriers are things like lack of self-confidence, self-doubt, or that inner voice that says, "You are not good enough."

External barriers are things like the Good Old Boys Club and organizational policies or politics that prevent women from moving up the corporate ladder or getting to be the head of the volunteer organization where they volunteer their time to help the community.

Joan C. Williams, in partnership with the Lean In Organization, came up with a series of video vignettes to address several gender biases or patterns.[2]

Here are the four gender biases Joan discovered in her research. I find her points very interesting since I experienced every one of these biases in my career.

1. Women have to prove it again and again and again.
2. Women walk the tightrope. If they are too feminine, they are not seen as a serious candidate for a senior-level position; if they are too masculine, they are seen as aggressive and bossy and not likeable.

---

2 You can check out Joan's video and find links to videos and discussion guides on my Kicking Glass Facebook page at https://www.facebook.com/womenkickingglass2.

3. The maternal wall. Once women become mothers, questions arise on their commitment level and willingness to do the job or relocate. Interestingly, this pattern stretches to women without children. Women without children are impacted too with questions about when they plan to have children.

4. The tug-of-war. Tug-of-war comes into play when the three items above come into conflict with one another.

One of the things women can do right now to help themselves and other women succeed is find a mentor and be a mentor to other women. We don't necessarily need our own version of the Good Old Boys Club, but we can help support and mentor other women.

One of my mentors in my early days at Microsoft is a perfect example of women helping women. Her name was Susan. When I joined Microsoft, my boss greeted me my first day, showed me to my office, took me to lunch, and then left on vacation for three weeks. Before he left, he gave me a list of ten people to meet who could help me "fit in." One of the people on the list was Susan.

Susan took me under her wing and introduced me to the important people on the team. She would explain that I joined because of my background and talent. Susan took me to every one of her meetings so I could meet the right people and start to learn the business.

Susan made sure to introduce me to our department general manager so I could get exposure to the top people in our business unit. I even participated in the company's big annual business meeting, and my GM introduced me to the top management of the company, including Bill Gates, Steve Ballmer, and the other executives.

In addition, I got to watch a great leader in action up close and personal. After my manager returned, Susan continued to mentor me and ask for me to be on all her special projects, including working on the company's worldwide sales and marketing conference. Thanks to Susan, I was connected to the right people at the top. She allowed me to shine beneath her wings.

One of the female leaders I read about, admire, and follow, as mentioned earlier, is Sheryl Sandberg with her groundbreaking book, *Lean In*. I'll mention Sheryl's work a couple of times in this book because I think she discovered some interesting things in her research on female leaders. Sheryl provides concrete examples of what women can do to be better leaders. She also founded the Lean In movement, and I encourage you to find a local chapter and join to learn from other great women.

Sheryl was a senior leader at Google, and yet when she was negotiating for her new job at Facebook, she had some moments of doubt about her capability as a leader. She had second thoughts about how much money she should negotiate and settle for when discussing her salary. Even Sheryl struggled with her internal barriers and questioned her worth.

Sheryl suggested ways women can demonstrate their leadership strengths by such things as arriving at a meeting a few minutes early and taking a seat at the main table in the room. Most meeting rooms have a large table in the middle with a few extra chairs. The research shows the people at the table are more likely to be recognized and their opinions heard than the people who sit along the sides of the room.

Sheryl recently had to dig deep to maintain her positive attitude and personal leadership strength. Her husband and soul mate had passed away recently after a tragic accident while on vacation in Mexico. Sheryl talked about her struggle to recover and deal with life as a single mother. She said one of the things that kept her going was the company of the women in her life.

Because of her recent struggle, she added a new component to the Lean In movement this year. The new movement is called Lean In Together and is about women helping women succeed in all parts of our lives.

Find a Small Group of Women to Support Each Other

We're getting ready to take over the world. My
group of girlfriends—we're renegades!
—LISA BONET

I have a group with three other women. We worked together early in our careers at Microsoft. Despite the fact we only technically worked together for a year or eighteen months in the same business unit, we stuck together and helped each other out from time to time. We've remained friends for over eighteen years and still keep in touch today.

Deb, my favorite boss, who helped me land a great job in our Asia Pacific region. She helped me throughout my career and provided valuable coaching and advice even though I did not work for her.

Yvonne is a special friend. We worked together on a very challenging project to train the entire Enterprise sales force in a new customer-centric sales methodology. We had a very small team and needed to train over eight thousand salespeople and their managers in eighteen months.

I had the US region, which included Latin America; Yvonne had Asia; and our other teammate, Mike, had Europe. We exceeded all of the goals set in front of us, and Yvonne and I developed a great friendship.

There were times Yvonne would e-mail or call from some remote part of Asia, just looking for someone to talk to who spoke English. Yvonne and I had different styles, but they complemented each other because we had a common vision and a common set of values or beliefs.

Yvonne was very helpful for me in staying balanced. She would tell me when I moved into what I call the "too zone"—when one of my strengths, like being assertive and stating my opinion, became "too aggressive" and I was being "too aggressive." Yvonne would hold my strength of being creative and loving change to being too random and spontaneous.

I remember one day, we both showed up to work in the exact same outfit in different colors. Yvonne's outfit was pink and mine was a light lavender. We thought it was so funny that we both showed up on the same day and in the exact same outfit. We walked around our floor and would walk into someone's office and start a conversation.

We stood there and had a business conversation until the other person noticed our matching outfits. When the person said, "Do you know you two have on the same outfit?" we would laugh our heads off and tell him or her we were twins.

The fourth member of our group was Arch'na. During my leave of absence and my personal healing time, I was doing a lot of things to help get myself back on track. I've always worked out at home, and I started doing cardio ballet workouts at home with a set of DVDs I bought online.

At one point, I started to feel better and decided I needed to get back in contact with the real world and get out of the house to interact with people other than my husband and family. Barre workouts are a combination of ballet, Pilates, and yoga and are probably the hardest workouts I've ever done.

I found a Groupon coupon for a discount at a local barre class less than a mile from my house. I signed up and started my first class. The first friendly, smiling face I saw in line was Arch'na. We had not worked together for over ten years, but our friendship and caring for each other came back immediately.

We helped each other since we were both going through a career transition, trying to find our next adventure. I enjoyed reconnecting with Arch'na and renewing our friendship.

A few months after reconnecting with each other, we started to have fun and casual dinners every month or so. We would eat dinner at nice restaurants, enjoy our martinis or wine, and laugh our heads off over all the challenging and fun times we have had together.

One night, Yvonne arranged a nice dinner at a new place in Issaquah, Washington, just outside of Seattle. We were having one of our usual fun evenings and laughing loudly about all of our challenges helping lead a sales and service culture change at work.

One of us spotted a male boss we had all worked with at different times across the room. We laughed, and someone said, "Let's go say hi to Steve together and see what he says."

Steve was having dinner with his wife, and we all knew her too, so we felt safe marching across the restaurant to talk to Steve as a team.

We all walked together across the room and stood at his table. He finally looked up and said, "I can't take all this woman power at once." We all made some smart comment and enjoyed a good laugh with Steve and his wife.

Let's take a look at what makes a great leader and what skills you need to be a great female leader like the women in my life.

CHAPTER 4

SO, WHAT IS A LEADER?

L et's start with some fundamental concepts on leadership in general. Then we'll dive into more specifics about female leaders, what they do, and how they manage their careers.

I have a number of odd habits, one of which is I love to look up the roots of words and where they come from. It helps me to understand the true meaning of the words or things around me. For example, let's look at the food artichokes. Who in their right mind hundreds of years ago looked at this ugly thistle brush with sharp points all around it and thought, "I should eat this"?

Who thought of the idea to cut down this ugly and hard-to-eat vegetable and decided it was a good source of nutrition? Who came up with the idea to boil it in water for a long time and then dip it in melted butter, mayonnaise, or a sauce? Who taught other people how to eat the artichokes by dragging the internal leaves over their teeth and eating it?

There has been a lot of discussion in the business world around whether people need to be leaders or managers in today's turbulent environment. So I decided I wanted to understand the word "leader" and the word "manager." I looked up "leader" in the dictionary to satisfy this odd habit of mine.

"Leader" comes from the Latin word *led*, which means "to determine the course of a ship." Here are some of the more detailed definitions of the word "leader" from the dictionary.

"The person or persons who are in charge of a group."
"The person or persons who lead a musical group."
"Someone who is responsible for a group or team."

There are two basic types of leaders. There are leaders who have positional power to lead a group; they usually have a job or title like manager, team leader, or director. There are also leaders who have influencer power. These types of leaders have a strong influence over other events even if they do not have formal positional power or a fancy job title.

When you look up the root meaning of the word "manager," you find it ultimately comes from the Latin word *manus* for "hand." It means to be hands-on. Here are some of the more detailed definitions of the word "manager."

> "Someone who is in charge of a business, department, etc."
> "Someone who directs the training and performance of a sports team."
> "Someone who directs the professional career of an entertainer or athlete."

I don't want to get into a big discussion over whether leaders or managers are better since in today's world, you need to use more leadership skills to help direct change than managerial skills to manage or control things. Warren Bennis, the great business guru, said, "Managers do things right, and leaders do the right things."

The fact is, in today's turbulent world of constant whitewater-type changes, you need to be more of a great leader and less of a great manager. Operating in today's business climate is like being on a river with one series of whitewater rapids after another. Just as things calm down, another wave of change can hit your business or you as a leader and knock you out of the boat or off course.

Many years ago, I used to do a lot of whitewater river rafting. It was a fun way to be outside in nature and in a place few people had a chance to visit. We would camp alongside the river at night and cook our meals over campfires, including pineapple upside down cake, which we baked in a cast-iron skillet over the coals.

On our first river rafting experience with a group of about twelve friends and strangers, the river guide was explaining how to row and work together as a team to have a safe and fun ride. At one point, he said, "When you fall out of the boat..."

I immediately raised my hand and like Delta Burke out of the old sitcom, *Designing Women,* said, "Excuse me. What do you mean *when* we fall out of the boat? Don't you mean *if* we fall out of the boat?"

I was quickly corrected and told the right way not to drown and get back in the boat. The instructions were to keep your head up, look downstream to see what was coming ahead, stay calm, and find a more peaceful part of the river to wait for the boat to catch up to you to save you.

Not bad advice for staying calm and dealing with the constant change every business and leader faces today. One of the fun parts of river rafting is as soon as you safely make your way through one set of rapids, you start to hear the roar of the water for the next rapid.

The message is change is here to stay, and leaders and businesses have to learn to adapt to change quickly so they can prepare for the next change.

Let me give you a couple of examples of the pace and impact of changes in businesses that have been around for a long time. Let's take a quick look at two specific examples. One is the taxicab industry, which has been around since the horse and buggy days. The industry had not changed for hundreds of years until a small upstart company named Uber came along.

The story goes that Uber was founded by two men who after a pleasant dinner in Paris late at night could not find a cab to get back to their hotel. They stood on the corner with their phones and tried to get a cab. One of the two men said, "Wouldn't it be great if we could use our phone to call a cab, be able to see the car as well as the license plate, and see a picture of the driver so we get in the right cab and home safely?"

Uber changed the cab industry forever, and now traditional taxi companies are trying to become more "Uber-like." Within six months of Uber's success, another upstart company, Lyft, came along. Lyft's original business model was geared more to women and, especially, female business travelers.

The second big Uber-like change can be seen in the camera and photography business. Kodak has been around for years and always had a competitive edge over their competition. They were in the traditional photo business with a camera, paper photos, and development in a store like CVS.

Kodak almost missed the digital photo era but managed to catch up a little. They were completely blindsided by the age of digital camera photos, Instagram, and Snapchat. The interesting thing is Kodak was presented with the idea of digital photos and chose to ignore it.

There are hundreds of examples of these kinds of changes in every industry. So what does this have to do with being a strong female leader? This means leaders of all kinds, men and women, need to learn to adapt to change. Leaders need a strong vision and set of values to serve as a foundation for their leadership journey. This means we need to learn new things and be willing to let go of the things that no longer work.

When the world shifts because of a new innovation, there is no going back. Do you want to go back to the days when you wasted a ton of money on bad vacation photos because you could not see which pictures were good or bad?

Are Leaders Made or Born?

There has been a lot of debate over the last thirty years on whether leaders are made or born. There certainly are women and men who were born to be leaders or raised in an environment where their leadership skills were encouraged, praised, and allowed to grow. The good news is that leadership skills can be taught and learned.

You can attend a training seminar, read a book, or watch a video on how to be a great leader. You can learn from the leaders in your life, good and bad. You can learn from life's lessons by observing things around you and learning from every life experience.

My good friend and fellow author, Laura Steward, wrote an amazing book (which I mentioned earlier) called, *What Would a Wise Woman Do?* about the questions we ask ourselves or should be asking ourselves as we move through life and become great leaders.

For example, when something happens to you, good or bad, ask yourself a series of questions.

1. What happened?
3. What did I do right in this situation?

4. What did I learn from this experience?
5. What do I need to do differently to create a different result next time?

These simple questions help us remove some of the emotion and pain of the moment and look at how we can learn from it. A great quote from Albert Einstein, the famous scientist is, "Doing the same thing over and over again and expecting a different result is the definition of insanity."

Trust me; doing this is hard at first and may even seem a little strange. I've put this practice to use many times in my life, usually when things have not gone so well. Sometimes it might take several hours, days, or months to break away from the emotion or pain, but using these types of questions can help minimize some of the emotion and pain; plus, you might be able to learn from it.

I recall times in my life when something bad or negative happened to me and I used this approach. I remember sitting in my car at the beach and going through the questions. Sometimes I would look to the sky and say, "God, if I am supposed to learn something from this event, can you please give me a hint?" Eventually, I would figure out the life lesson and move on.

CHAPTER 5

LEADERS IN YOUR LIFE

People won't remember what you say,
people won't remember what you do,
people will remember how you made them feel!
—MAYA ANGELOU

Here is an exercise for you to reflect on the leaders in your life. Think for a moment about the person or people who influenced you in your life and helped you become the person you are today. It might have been your mother or father. It might have been your old soccer coach or band leader. It might have been a teacher, preacher, or famous leader you read about in school. It might have been a boss or manager who was a wonderful mentor to you.

Ask yourself the following questions:

1. Who had the biggest impact on my life and helped form who I am today?
2. How did he or she influence me growing up?
3. How does he or she influence me today?

This person (or these people) was a leader in your life. He or she probably did not have positional power but did have the power to lead you and help you become the person you are today.

Whatever your position in life, whatever your chosen path—a career woman or a stay-at-home mom—don't forget the leaders in your life. Remember these leaders had someone who helped them become the person they became or wanted to be. Don't you want to pass this on to someone in your life?

So, here is the big question as you read this book and embark on your leadership journey. What kind of leader do you want to be?

This book is a collection of stories, best practices, and practical exercises to help you develop self-mastery, play to your strengths, and be the best you can be. I'll cite several other books by authors I know, admire, and recommend you read as well.

Many books written to help women leaders are great and are full of helpful advice, but I wanted this book to be a little different. I wanted this book to provide practical applications of the best practices I collected from my personal experiences and the ones I've read about or heard about from other leaders.

In the remainder of this book, I'll share my other findings, stories, and examples of what women have done and tell you what you can do to become the kind of leader you want to be in your chosen professional and personal life.

Practical Application and Leadership Action Plan—Part 1

1. Complete this exercise to determine the leaders in your life who helped form you and the person you've become.
   a. Think of the person or people who had the biggest impact or influence on your life.

   b. Picture this person or these people in your mind.

   c. Who were they?

   d. What did they do to influence or impact you?

   e. How do they still influence you and help you be the person you are today?

Remember this person or these people as you go through the remainder of this book.

SECTION 1

MY LEADERSHIP JOURNEY

You held me down, but I got up
Already brushing off the dust
You hear my voice, you hear that sound
Like thunder, gonna shake the ground

You held me down, but I got up
Get ready 'cause I've had enough
I see it all, I see it now

I got the eye of the tiger, a fighter
Dancing through the fire
'Cause I am the champion, and you're gonna hear me roar
Louder, louder than a lion!
—KATY PERRY, "ROAR"

CHAPTER 6

MY STORY—THE EARLY DAYS

The best and most beautiful things in the world cannot be
seen or even touched—they must be felt with the heart!
—HELEN KELLER

As I mentioned earlier, my family was a normal middle-class family with a dad who worked at one company his entire career and a stay-at-home mom. I credit my mom with giving me the gift of her tenacity and sense of humor. I credit my dad for raising me in a sports-oriented family and helping me understand how sports can help you later in life. Don't get me wrong; you don't have to be a jock or sports fanatic to succeed in business. Maybe you grew up with a passion for music or books that helped you in your life.

I started playing tennis at the age of seven and continued to play through high school, college, and later in life. The times my dad and I would play tennis or enter tournaments are some of my favorite memories. One of my favorite stories about my dad was the time he was trying to teach me to play net in tennis. He tied a rope around my waist and to the net to teach me how to hang in there. I was afraid to play the net, or stand close to the net, for fear of being hit. I would stand at the back of the court and rarely approached the net.

With tears streaming down my face, my dad hit a bucket of tennis balls at me until I learned to stay tough and stand my ground. Today, this simple act would be considered child abuse, but to my dad and me, it was a lesson of love.

I did pretty well in school and had a lot of good friends and memories. I was active in school sports and the usual social activities, like attending football games, joining clubs, and being part of school leadership activities. My group of friends would go to every football, basketball, track, or swimming event. After each event, we would go to King Arthur's Pizza in Rialto, California.

My family moved around a lot because of my dad's job. Dad worked hard and many times would work different shifts. I went to six different elementary schools in six years. I think one of the reasons I like to change and do things differently and make contacts and friends easily is that I had to make friends fast because we moved so much.

My mom would adjust when we would have dinner, depending on whether he was working days, mid-shifts, or nights. One of my favorite things to do when my dad worked the night shift was to wake him up for dinner. I would quietly open the door and let in a little light and then gently wake him up.

I used to help Mom by packing my dad's lunch. If I wanted something like a new tennis racket, I would put notes in my dad's lunch or cut a picture of the exact tennis racket I wanted out of the newspaper and put it in instead. I usually got the tennis racket or the special thing I wanted.

One of the funny things that happened at my wedding many years later was my dad shook my new husband's hand and said, "Good luck. She's expensive."

My College and Early Careers

I went to college with the goal of becoming a teacher and graduated with honors. I was excited upon graduation to be hired by North Torrance School District to teach history and economics. My excitement only lasted six months. The State of California passed a new law called Proposition 13, which limited the amount California home owners paid in property taxes. Sounds great, right? Well, it was great if you were a home owner, but bad if you were a new teacher, just starting out in your career. The result of this proposition being passed was that all new teachers were laid off to save money.

Here I was, twenty-one years old, a recent college grad with no job, no career, and no money. My first thought was, whom do I know who can help me land a job fast? I immediately thought of a close family friend who was a senior vice president at a big bank.

This close family friend helped me land a job as a teller at one of the branches he had worked at for twenty years. I went to work for the bank because I needed a job and found I loved banking. I progressed quickly from a teller to an operations manager and branch manager.

After about five years with this large bank, I realized if I was ever going to get back to my passion of teaching, I needed to move to a smaller bank where I had the opportunity to move into training or human resources. I took a job that was basically a "lateral move," meaning I took a similar job for only a little bit more money to get in the door or in order to gain an experience I thought would help me move closer to the job I really wanted.

After I had worked about a year as an operations manager, a job came open for a field trainer. I did not know what a field trainer was, but I knew I would be training managers in the branches and local offices to be better managers. I wanted to be teaching again, so I went for the job.

I drove to downtown LA for the first time and got completely lost driving and walking. When I finally found the parking garage and parked my car, I got out and tried to find the building. I looked at all these very tall skyscrapers and could not find the bank tower for my final interview.

Well, I finally found the building, had a great interview, and landed the job. I was so excited that I was finally going to be doing the work I loved—training and teaching people to reach their full potential. I did not have the details, but I made the decision with my heart to pursue my dream. For all I knew at the time, being a field trainer meant I would be training corn to stand in neat rows.

I went back to my office to tell my manager about my exciting news. His response surprised me; he tried to talk me out of taking the job. In his view, moving to a headquarters role was a bad career choice and I should stay with him and become a branch manager just like him.

One of my first lessons as a female leader is don't let other people tell you what is best for you. Becoming a branch manager of a small branch and then a medium-sized or bigger branch was the last thing I wanted to do. I trusted my instincts and went with my gut that this was the right decision for me.

I stayed with this bank and moved up the ranks to become a vice president of the Center for Customer and Employee Excellence in our Southern California Division. Again, I loved the job and had the chance to learn a lot and work on some great projects with great people. I had a chance to work on a great project to help the bank stay competitive in the face of a government deregulation initiative to allow savings and loans to offer the same services as banks.

I remember one time being in a big meeting at the corporate headquarters in downtown LA. When I walked into the room and looked around, I saw a meeting room filled with white, middle-aged men who all looked alike in their blue or gray suits with button-down shirts and ties.

At the time, the trend in banking for women was to try to dress like the men. So, I showed up in my navy-blue blazer and white button-down shirt with a little bow tie folded to look like a rose.

After being in the room for over two and a half hours, I needed to go to the bathroom. I quietly got up and started to walk toward the bathroom. One of those middle-aged white males looked at me walking toward the door and loudly said, "Where are you going, young lady?"

I responded, "I am going to the bathroom. I'll be back in less than two minutes."

He looked at me, confused, and said, "We don't take breaks in these meetings. We don't want to lose the momentum of the meeting and slow things down."

My response was, "Well, I can pee here or I can pee in the bathroom. Which do you prefer?" I looked him in the eye and said, "Watch me." I walked out the door, came back less than two minutes later, and proceeded to participate in the meeting.

I helped lead my Southern California Division of 110 branches through a major culture-change effort to become a customer- and sales-oriented bank. This project was a blast. We changed everything—the structure of the traditional branch, job descriptions, recognition and reward systems, and communications systems—and retrained everyone from senior leaders to branch managers and frontline tellers.

As part of my leadership development, I attended a fantastic five-day off-site leadership training program conducted by the Center for Creative Leadership. Part of the workshop included a 360-degree assessment of my leadership skills and several different personal style and learning style assessments. Attending this class was part of my professional development, and in the end, it changed my life.

I learned a lot about myself and realized while I loved working at the bank, it was not really allowing me to fully live my dream and vision and pursue my passion. The last day of the training, they had us go to our favorite place to write out our personal and professional plan for our future. I always found that my favorite and most creative place was outside by water.

So I found a nice lounge chair by the pool and started to write out my personal, professional, and spiritual life plan. I wrote for hours and wrote out my top professional goal was to leave the bank by the end of the year. I wanted to pursue my passion to help teach leaders and teams to be the best they could be full time. I had no desire to take the traditional career route in banking, moving up the corporate ladder in the usual way.

After the training, I returned to work at the bank and started to make contact with people I knew could help me find this type of consulting and leadership-training work when I left the bank and started my own training and consulting firm.

I contacted the people I worked with to develop many of the management classes I'd been delivering at the bank for the last ten years. I went to my senior vice president (SVP) and head of human resources and told him my plan to leave the bank by the end of the year. I asked if he would hire me back to teach the five-day off-site leadership course, which we offered in Santa Barbara once a month to senior leaders and frontline managers.

Three interesting things happened. First, everyone I talked to was willing to help me and told me the bank would be happy to hire me back to deliver this awesome program. The overwhelming response was "Yes, we would be happy to help."

Second, my senior vice president went to one of my good friends, John, a fellow vice president, and asked him what he could do to keep me at the bank. John told my SVP that there was nothing he could do and no job offer he could make me that would keep me at the bank. John told him to let me go and take advantage of my talent as a trainer to teach our managers to be better leaders.

Third, my dad, who always taught me I could do anything I put my mind to, was shocked I was leaving the bank and a safe, lifelong career in banking to start my own business. You see, my dad only worked at one company for thirty-five years, and he could not understand why I would leave what he considered a great and honorable career to start my own company.

Wow...what an interesting life lesson from these events! I learned to follow my passion. I've always told people, including my kids, "Do what you love, and the money will follow."

Here is another interesting thing that happened to me. I wrote my personal, professional, and spiritual plan in May with the goal of leaving the bank by the end of the year. I left the bank on September 15, over three months ahead of my goal of leaving by the end of the year. The funny or ironic thing is I wrote my exit and new business plan down in May, put it away, and did not look at until a year later when I had exceeded my goal.

I always heard about various studies of college graduates who left a great college like Harvard. Those who had a clear plan, which was written down, were far more successful than their fellow students who did not have a clear goal or plan. The power of the connection between the mind and a written plan proved true for me. Later in this book, I'll have you work on your personal, professional, and life plan too.

Taking the Leap and Leaving the Corporate World

I managed, led, and facilitated the awesome five-day off-site program for the bank and continued to expand my business with other clients. I successfully ran my consulting company for over ten years. At the time, we were living in California, and my husband decided to go help run a family business in Kirkland, Washington, just outside of Seattle.

My husband and I tried living in two different cities and traveling back and forth once a month. We had a young son, Ross Montgomery

Grimm III, who was six at the time. Ross III stayed in California, and my husband, Ross Jr., moved to Kirkland to live with his mom and run the business.

After about eighteen months of this bi-state relationship, we made the decision that Ross III and I should move to Kirkland and be with Ross for the good of the family. So we packed everything we owned into a moving van and moved to Kirkland the day after Christmas. We flew Ross III to Seattle to stay with my husband's family while Ross and I drove the moving van to Kirkland in one of the snowiest winters in history.

Heading north, we knew the snow in the mountains between California, Oregon, and Washington could be very bad, so we decided to head for the coast to avoid the worst of the snow. Well, just as we reached the coast of Oregon, we hit black ice and almost spun out the moving van. We decided to stop at a motel for the night and pick up our journey in the morning with better light.

When we finally arrived in Kirkland and started to unload the van, we found out that a lot of stuff was frozen in place. We unpacked and moved in the snow. We moved in with my amazing mother-in-law, Gigi, and remained there for the first year.

I can honestly say my mother-in-law was the most amazing, loveliest, and strongest woman. She worked as the head of critical care at the Fred Hutchinson Cancer Unit in Seattle. In order for someone to be admitted to Fred Hutchinson, they had to be diagnosed with life-threatening cancer.

My mother-in-law is a small, petite woman who only stands five feet tall, and yet she would lift patients and help give the patients the care they needed to be comfortable. When she retired, she was honored by the medical industry as a top caregiver. The letters from patients and families made everyone cry when they talked about how Gigi had helped them through the difficult part of their lives.

One of the funny stories about this amazing woman, who was a true leader in her field, was when we were moving into her house, I found what looked like a brick in the freezer wrapped in foil. When I asked her what it was, she told me it was medical marijuana for her patients. At the time, possessing marijuana was illegal. I dropped the package at first and then carefully put it back in the freezer.

For the next five years, I flew back to California to work with my clients every week. I would leave on Monday morning at 6:00 a.m. on Alaska Airlines and fly to Orange County and then back on Thursday night or Friday morning.

I flew so often I knew every pilot and flight attendant on the route. At one point, I was contacted by Alaska Airlines and the *Wall Street Journal*, who wanted to write an article about me since I was the first woman to rack up one million miles on Alaska Airlines and this was in the days Alaska Airlines only flew up and down the West Coast. I became a million-mile club member and lifetime MVP of Alaska Airlines' mileage program, which has some nice benefits. The downside was I spent a lot of time on planes away from my family.

At one point, I felt I was living the movie *Planes, Trains, and Automobiles*, with Steve Martin and John Candy. In the movie, Steve Martin is a businessman who is stuck in a city far from home and trying to get back to his family. John Candy is trying to help him get home through a series of very funny failed attempts via a plane, a train, and finally an automobile.

My goal every week was to be home for the weekend to be with my family for a few days of quality time before I flew on to the next city. I was in Alma, Michigan, at an oil refinery client where the plant was so bad I shared an office with the Environmental Protection Agency (EPA). It was the dead of winter, and I could not get my usual one-stop flight home on Friday.

I was literally crying at the ticket counter, trying to get home for my son's little league football game. The agent was trying to help me, but the only way I could get home was to drive to Detroit in my rental car in a snowstorm since the local airport was snowed in, hope to get a plane out of Detroit, catch a flight to Denver, and then take a flight from Denver to Salt Lake City and finally a flight from Salt Lake City to Seattle.

Well, I made the flights and got home at 9:00 a.m. the next day on Saturday morning in time for my son's game. The joys of business travel.

I meet many people who tell me how they would love to travel around the world like I have. I know it sounds fun, exciting, and glamorous, and it is—at first. But after traveling for more than thirty years, I found the job of business travel lost its luster. Don't get me wrong; I've seen some of the most beautiful places in the world from Germany, Australia, and New Zealand to Thailand, but it got really old and lonely.

Here is my basic business travel pattern. I would sit in the car to the airport, work in the hotel and office, eat at some restaurant usually alone, go back to my room to do e-mail, and then head back to the office. Rinse and repeat in the next country.

My husband, Ross, and I have been married for over thirty-four years. We often joke that the reason we've stayed married for so long is that we were seldom in the same city long enough to fight too much. If we had a fight on Sunday or Monday, by the time I got back on Friday or Saturday, we'd forgotten what we were fighting about and it probably didn't matter in the end. I was just glad to be home with family again.

My Fall from the Top of the Corporate Ladder

I was lucky enough to be at the right time and in the right place in 1998 to be hired by Microsoft. I was hired to help transform Microsoft into a more customer-centric and professional sales organization. I had many wonderful experiences, worked with some of the world's smartest people, and had some incredible jobs. I love the company, and after I left in 2013, they continued to hire me as a sales-enablement consultant. I still deliver sales-leadership and sales-strategy programs around the world.

Arianna Huffington talks about her "fall" in her book *Thrive*. She shares her story of how after years of being a top performer and a top-level executive, she was so exhausted one night that she woke up when her head hit her computer. She literally fell asleep working too hard. She broke her cheek and had to go to the hospital.

One of her aha moments, which she talks about in her book (I highly recommend you read it), was something as simple as she needed to sleep more. Yes, the most important thing she recommends is sleep. Arianna frequently speaks about the importance of sleep to help people be more productive and effective and healthier.

My own fall was not as physically damaging, but it was just as profound and potentially damaging to my health and my life. Around 2009, I started to notice a dramatic shift and drop in my productivity and in both my personal and professional lives. I started to feel bad, tired, and simply exhausted most of the time.

Here was my typical day. I would wake up at 5:30 a.m., grab a cup of coffee, and do a quick workout. I would check my e-mail, which usually increased to several hundred new e-mails overnight. I would head to the office around 8:00 a.m. or so and try to do my job. I would leave the office around 6:00 p.m. to head home for dinner. Literally right after dinner, I would be back on e-mail until around 9:00 p.m. or 10:00 p.m. I worked almost every weekend, and if I didn't work on Saturday, I felt guilty and worked all day Sunday.

This pattern went on for years. The job I used to love became a chore. I noticed I did not have the same passion, and I am sure it showed. Most days, I felt like I was walking in molasses on a cold Montana winter night. My hair started to fall out, and I gained thirty-five pounds rather quickly.

It got so bad that I would send a short e-mail to someone, and when I would read it later, it made no sense since I left words out or used the wrong word, which changed the context of the message.

I was completely lost, and I lost my sense of who I was, what I stood for, and what I loved to do. I lost touch with family and friends because I was too busy to attend events, and if I did attend, I was never totally present. I became a shell of myself. The things I loved to do—like read a good book, listen to music, and cook—were gone.

I loved to cook and entertain for a few friends, but it got so bad, I felt like I no longer knew how to cook or even grocery shop. I would make a list of things to get at the store. I would go to the store and forget two or three things on the list I had in my hand.

Even cooking stressed me out. I would read the recipe several times and still do things in the wrong order. Luckily, for most of the recipes, it did not matter if I put the flour in before the salt, but for some, it did.

I started going to a series of doctors and nurse practitioners for help. They all told me the same thing. I was suffering from a case of extreme fatigue and exhaustion and was probably depressed. I was in complete denial and kept trying to push my way through the muck. I was always a top performer and received a number of special awards. People used to describe me as the Energizer Bunny because I was always moving and so happy. How could I, of all people, be depressed?

One of the doctors gave me a prescription to treat the depression, but it did not make me feel any better. In fact, I was paranoid about taking the medication. Those commercials we all see about the side effects of every drug on the face of the earth scared the heck out of me. I believed all of them.

Finally, after about two years of trying to push through and buck up, I called the Employee Assistance Program at Microsoft and was referred to a counselor. I went to see her twice a week in the beginning and once a week after a month or so. Remember, I loved this company and still do. I wanted to get well and get back to work as fast as possible.

The counselor had me read a wonderful book by Louise Hay, *You Can Change Your Life*. This book and the exercises probably did change and save my life. I highly recommend this book to the women I know since it had such a positive impact on my life.

I read the book and did every exercise, including telling myself I loved myself and I was worthy. I wrote down everything I was grateful for, kept a journal, and started saying positive affirmations to myself several times a day. I felt very silly at first, but over time, I started to enjoy it.

One activity this counselor suggested to help me was the vision board. She gave me a piece of construction paper and a bunch of magazines and asked me to cut and paste pictures of my ideal life on the board. I cut out pictures of families, people smiling, flowers, scenes at the beach, people working out, trees, oceans, and so on.

I realized through this exercise, for the first time, that I had stopped living my vision and let work interfere with my true passions. I started to walk my adorable pug, Roxie, through the woods by my house, listening to inspirational songs like "I Think I Can Fly" by R. Kelly, "Stronger" by Kelly Clarkson, and "Girl on Fire" by Alicia Keys.

At one point, the counselor told me that the job was probably going to put me in the hospital or possibly kill me. She recommended I see a great female psychologist to determine if I needed to take a leave of absence and get my life back in order.

I went to see the doctor on a Friday afternoon at two. She sat me down, asked me a few questions, and had me take a couple of tests. After she scored the tests, she told me I was on a medical leave of absence immediately. She forbade me to call my office or tell them anything about what was going on and why I was on going on a mandatory medical leave of absence. She said she would contact the right people in HR to get the process started.

I cried all the way home. When I finally got home, I was sobbing so hard my husband could not understand what I was saying. I finally calmed down, and he reassured me everything would be fine and we would figure out how to get through this together.

Here's how much I loved the company and still wanted to do a good job. Despite my doctor's orders, I called my manager and asked him to meet me someplace away from our building. Before I went to the doctor that day, I had been working on a video project for a big upcoming event. I had my boss meet me at the Microsoft Studio where I was secretly working and editing a video that day. Remember, the doctor had forbidden me to go to work, but I did anyway. I could not leave my manager and team hanging.

Before I met with my manager, I wrote a report on every project I was working on, including the current status and what still needed to be done. After handing off my project list to my wonderful and understanding manager, I went home and started to work on myself for the first time in many years.

I spent the next four months taking care of myself. I tried to focus on my mind and my body. I worked out, read self-improvement books, tried to meditate, and kept a daily journal. I honestly think I am meditation-challenged. I've tried to do the deep breathing and long meditation sessions, and I simply can't do it. The best I can do is ten to fifteen minutes of quiet breathing before my mind starts racing around to the ten things I need to get done that day.

I needed to figure out what I was going to do for the rest of my life and find my passion again. I found a great professional coach in Seattle named Patty, who was a fellow rower. She rowed in college, and I was part of the Singapore American dragon-boat team when I lived in Singapore for Microsoft. We had a lot in common, and I liked her no-nonsense, practical approach.

She had me do a number of exercises. The first one, which I'll have you complete at the end of the section, was to do a life chart. She gave me a circle with eight categories, like career, work, free time, fitness, and so on. The instructions were to complete the pie chart with either the number of hours or time I dedicated to each area.

I am sure I already knew this in my mind, but putting it on paper was a real eye-opener. I was basically spending 75 percent or more of my time working. I did not have time for friends, personal development, volunteer work, or doing things that I loved. My life was so out of balance that when people would ask me what I did on any given weekend, my response was, "I worked."

Another exercise was like the TV show *Let's Make a Deal.* I was trying to decide whether I wanted to try to return to Microsoft full time at the end of my leave, find another job, or restart the management consulting firm I owned for over ten years before I went to work for Microsoft.

She gave me a piece of paper with the instructions for the exercise I was to complete before our next session the following week. The exercise went something like this. She told me I had three doors in front of me, each one representing one of my three choices. For each door or choice, I was supposed to write down the pros and cons, including how I would tell my boss, my peers, my friends, and my family about my choice.

I chose door three, which was I would leave Microsoft as a full-time employee and restart my consulting practice. I went back to work at the end of my leave. My boss told me that in my absence, he had restructured the department to allow me to do what I did best. I thanked him and told him that he was a great manager but I had decided to leave Microsoft and pursue my passion. He understood and worked with HR to make it easy for me to leave with grace.

If you are planning a career or life choice, I recommend you do the same exercise to help you get clear about the options for you personally, professionally, financially, and spiritually.

Now is the time for you to take action on getting your life back or at least a little more into balance.

Personal Leadership Action Plan Part 2

Nothing is impossible; the word itself says, "I'm possible!"
—AUDREY HEPBURN, GROUNDBREAKING ACTRESS

If you are trying to make a decision about a career or life choice, try this exercise. Complete it as follows:

Step 1

Complete the following circle with the amount of time you are doing something that falls into that category. For example, how much time do you spend working at a job or volunteer project? Remember, being a mom is a job too. How much time do you spend sleeping? How much time do you spend on yourself or personal growth? Complete your circle, and remember everyone on the planet only has twenty-four hours a day and your total amount of time or percentage must add up to 100 percent, or twenty-four hours.

Remember, this is your life and you need to control your own life. We'll talk later in the book about what to do if you are feeling stuck or out of control, but for now, just focus on this exercise.

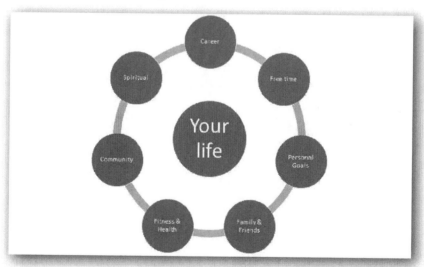

Step 2

For each area, write down one thing you are going to work on for the next thirty days to increase or decrease the amount of time you spend in each area. For example, "I'm going to increase my workouts by fifteen minutes a day" or "I am going to reduce the amount of time I spend on work by thirty minutes a day."

Research shows it takes twenty-eight days to change quite a bit. In fact, Sandra Bullock starred in a movie called *28 Days*. In the movie, she is an alcoholic in complete denial and needs to stay in this rehab center for twenty-eight days. Give yourself thirty days to change your one thing and then move on to another area to improve the balance in your life.

Complete the following life chart with your one thing for each area.

Career
Free time or play time
Personal goals or development
Physical or fitness
Financial goals
Community service
Spiritual

Questions to Ask Yourself

1. Are you happy with the current balance in your life?
2. Where do you need to spend more time to be more balanced?
3. Where do you need to spend less time to be more balanced?

Remember, your life chart will change depending on where you are in your career, and you can repeat this exercise anytime you feel out of balance. For example, when I was early in my career at the bank and my husband was a chief financial officer with a high-end hotel in Los Angeles, the work part of my chart was pretty big.

After I had my son, my life chart changed considerably. I had to be at the babysitter's by 6:00 p.m. or pay a large overtime fee. I could not stay in downtown Los Angeles a couple of times a week to have drinks and dinner with friends. I wanted to increase my family time and reduce my work time.

Step 3

Make informed choices.

Let's say you need to make an important personal or career choice. Maybe you are considering taking another job in another department or having a baby. This chart and approach really helped me make the tough decision to leave Microsoft after a great fifteen-year career.

Here is how to complete the exercise now if you are considering making a career or personal choice now or in the future. Do a pros-and-cons analysis for each choice using the following Career and Personal-Choice chart.

1. What would be the good things personally, professionally, financially, and spiritually for each choice, and what are the bad or negative things that can happen for each choice?
2. Make the decision or set a date in the near future to make your decision.

Career and Personal-Choice Chart

Choice 1	Choice 2	Choice 3
What are the pros or positives?	What are the pros or positives?	What are the pros or positives?
What are the cons or negatives?	What are the cons or negatives?	What are the cons or negatives?

Step 4

Develop your communication plan.

Now, develop your communication plan for your choice. What will you tell the people in your life about your choice? Write out the exact words you would say and practice them several times a day until you are ready.

What will you tell your family about your choice?

What will you tell your coworkers or other volunteers about your choice?

What will you tell your boss about your choice?

What will you tell new people you meet in the future about why you made this choice?

What will you tell yourself?

Remember, earlier I shared some questions to use to help you learn from every experience. Here is one practical application of using questions called an after-action review (AAR). Thirty days after your choice, ask yourself the following questions:

1. What happened?
2. What did I learn from it—good or bad?
3. What will I do next time to create a different result or outcome?

Repeat this same exercise every time you are faced with making a big or tough personal or professional decision. It works like magic, and you'll feel better about the choices you make.

I recovered from the fall and made a decision to restart my consulting company, write this book, and help another woman either avoid the fall or notice she is falling sooner than I did.

I spent the next several months writing in a journal, writing positive affirmations, and focusing on finding my voice and my best self. I started to relive my personal leadership vision, which is to *make a difference and empower people to reach their full potential.*

Control your own destiny; otherwise, someone else will. Why would you give that power to anyone? Have a plan, work your plan, and live your plan.

This is your life. Own it!

Tip: Always remember, life is a journey and be sure to enjoy the ride.

SECTION 2

BE STRONG

You think you got the best of me
Think you've had the last laugh
Bet you think that everything good is gone
Think you left me broken down
Think that I'd come running back
Baby, you don't know me, 'cause you're dead wrong

What doesn't kill you makes you stronger
Stand a little taller
Doesn't mean I'm lonely when I'm alone.
What doesn't kill you makes a fighter
Footsteps even lighter...
—KELLY CLARKSON, "STRONGER
(WHAT DOESN'T KILL YOU)"

CHAPTER 7

DEB'S STORY—BREAKING THROUGH AT WEST POINT

Never limit yourself because of others' limited imagination;
never limit others because of your own limited imagination.
—MAE DEMISON

One of the amazing women I interviewed early in my research study was Deb. She was one of the first women to attend and graduate from West Point, the prestigious US military academy. Until Deb and the other brave women broke through at West Point, the school was 100 percent a school for young men who wanted to go into the military.

In order for women to be able to attend West Point, everything had to change—there were no restrooms for women or sleeping dorms for the female students to stay in while they attended school. Deb told me about the many challenges she and her fellow female classmates had to endure not only to make it through the tough academic and physical demands but the personal challenges as well, including being treated differently because she was a woman and acts of sexual or other types of harassment.

Deb told me her strategy for graduating from West Point and becoming a high-ranking officer in the army was to develop a self-mastery approach to her schooling and career.

You see, many of these ground- or glass-breaking women had to learn a lot of stuff on their own. The male trainers would give the women the basics on how to perform a task, but in many cases, they were left to their own devices to figure it out. While male candidates got extra training or time with their trainers, the women were forced to master many of the skills on their own.

Deb felt she had to do better, be smarter, and work harder to be viewed as an equal to her male counterparts. She had to use her self-knowledge and self-mastery to succeed and in fact thrive in a thirty-year military career, leading large troops of men and women.

Deb took extra time to practice at every task or job put in front of her. There were some physical limitations she had to overcome since she was smaller, lighter, and not as fast or strong as some of the men, but she could be smarter and be a better leader.

The fact is her troops loved her because she was the kind of leader they wanted to follow. She excelled in every leadership assignment. She worked hard and learned what it took to be a great leader, and she put it all into practice.

The one sad thing is that the military has a thirty-year career limit, meaning people are forced to retire after thirty years unless there is some very special or unique situation that might extend a person's career by a few years. So after an amazing thirty-year career doing the work she loved, Deb was forced to retire.

One of the things I learned from Deb was to have an overall infinite winning mind-set in everything you do. Start every job or task with positive intentions and as a force for good. According to Deb—and I agree 100 percent—life is not a zero-sum game where one side wins and the other one loses.

In the military, survival lies in people collaborating and not competing with one another. Competing with a fellow recruit or officer could lead to someone being injured or killed. There is a saying in the military, "No soldier left behind."

The lessons for us as female leaders are that we need to help lift each other up and not tear each other down. We need to support other women and praise their accomplishments. We should never compete against each other but help each other move into the positions of leadership we desire.

As Deb said, "Never undercut, undermine, or attack anyone with anger or under any circumstances." If you need to correct someone's performance, do so in private and with dignity. I'll talk later in the book about one of the leaders I used to work for who believed the exact opposite of this type of thinking.

The following are Deb's seven leadership principles:

1. Lead from the heart. Maintain positive intent in everything you do.
2. Stay authentic and true to yourself, no matter what happens.
3. Love kindness. Find joy in life and the people around you.
4. Lead with quiet strength. Have high standards of honoring others.
5. Be openly vulnerable. See the goodness in others and stay open to possibilities.
6. Have a sense of humor. Practice self-deprecating humor versus humor at the expense of others.
7. Be a passionate learner. Stretch to new heights and reach for the stars.

Her final word of advice to other female leaders is to be a strong leader who makes a greater impact. In order to do so, you must be willing to put yourself out there, knowing the potential benefits are worth the imagined risks.

Good news, the last time I talked to Deb, she and her husband were happily living in Hawaii. It's a tough duty, but she earned it. Today, more and more women are accepted to West Point and serving our country because of women like Deb, who broke the concrete ceiling.

CHAPTER 8

SELF-KNOWLEDGE AND SELF-MASTERY—KEYS TO YOUR SUCCESS AS A LEADER

Everyone deserves the right to twinkle!
—MARILYN MOORE

In my humble opinion (IMHO), there are many keys to being an effective leader, but let's start with two very important ones. The first one is to develop self-mastery and self-knowledge. The second is to know your strengths and learn how to leverage your strengths, which we'll address in the next section.

Let's start with self-knowledge and self-mastery. Having self-knowledge without self-mastery is like being the best natural dancer in the world and never practicing your skills or never dancing at all. Having self-mastery without self-knowledge might mean that you are really great at something you don't like doing or don't enjoy.

Think of reading this book as your personal journey to discover your strengths and master your skills. Think about your life as a lifelong adventure where every day can be a powerful learning experience. In this section of the book, we'll be talking about and providing practical tactics and activities to help you *be strong*.

Probably one of the most famous sales gurus of the last fifty years is a gentleman named Zig Ziegler. Zig has written countless books and been an international speaker at thousands of conferences or training events. Zig could also be classified as the perfect example of an optimist since I don't know if Zig ever had two bad days in a row. One of my favorite quotes by Zig is "When you're green, you grow; when you're ripe, you rot." In other words, each one of us should be doing something every day to keep ourselves green and look at life as a lifelong learning opportunity.

Be very practical about your self-knowledge and personal mastery. For example, if you are not a morning person and can't seem to get things going before 10:00 a.m. and three cups of strong coffee, then plan your day around your natural peak performance patterns. (Later in the book, I do encourage people to try to become earlier risers. There is scientific proof of the benefits of adopting an early to bed, early to rise mentally.)

Face it, most people are either night owls or early risers. Very few people on this planet have a peak performance period that lasts all day long. If they do, they put 100 percent of their energy into their work during the day and go home exhausted with nothing to give in their personal life or family. Plan your day around your strengths, and schedule your daily routine during your peak performance periods.

When I worked as an operations manager at a bank in California, I had a teller named Barbie. Barbie was great with the customers, especially in the mornings up to just after the afternoon lunchtime rush. Toward the end of the day, Barbie would lose her concentration and start to make a lot of errors. Most of these errors were due to two things. One, Barbie got up very early and loved to work out before she came to work. The second challenge for Barbie was she started to get a bit sleepy after lunch. She would then make a lot of errors when counting money or completing her paperwork.

One day, Barbie was in a complete panic. She had made so many errors that at the end of the day when she counted out her money and tried to balance her teller account, she was close to a million dollars out of balance. I knew this was not possible and that the errors would correct themselves in the morning, but I had to call our regional headquarters to report the situation.

Sure enough, everything showed up the next day, and Barbie was only out of balance about ten dollars. After this rather scary event, I sat down with Barbie and asked her questions about her strengths, the things she liked to do, and the things she did not like to do. It turns out in addition to being an earlier riser, Barbie was scared to death of handling money. My solution was to move Barbie from being a teller to being a new-account representative where she could practice and use her great customer-service skills. Barbie excelled in her new role, and I slept a lot easier and never had to call the regional HQ for a teller being out of balance by a million dollars again.

One of my strengths has been organizing and running training events or conferences for my entire career. I started running women's learning events back in the late eighties. The first year, I hired a wonderful motivational speaker named Bobbi. I brought the women (and the few men) who worked at the back in non-officer positions (teller, new-accounts representatives, proof machine operators, and so on) to a nice hotel for a half-day workshop as a learning event to focus on building their self-esteem and helping them feel better about themselves.

At the end of the event, the women felt loved, motivated, and supported. As I started to plan the second event, people told me not to hire an outside speaker and pay him or her several thousand dollars but to save the money and be the main motivational speaker myself.

So I took the money I would have spent on a professional outside speaker and put it toward buying door prizes and nice gifts for the people attending. I bought TV sets, stereo boom boxes, gift baskets, and many other things to give away as door prizes for fun contests.

Most important, I found my passion to help people feel good about themselves. I love planning events. I love facilitating workshops and helping people discover their true talents. I was living my vision to *make a difference and empower people to reach their full potential.*

Most of my career, whether it was part of my core job or not, I always seemed to get pulled in to run these types of events. I've run hundreds of training events and conferences over the years and it is both one of my strengths and something I love doing. These events can range from five to ten people attending a women's networking breakfast to twenty-five thousand people attending a worldwide conference.

One of the ways I continued to increase my self-knowledge and self-mastery was volunteering to be on committees or volunteering to set up, run, and speak at these types of events. I also attended other conferences so I could learn how to run better and more impactful learning events.

Regardless of my role, I developed both a personal passion and expertise in this area and seemed to be asked to do these types of motivational or learning events frequently. Every role I've had for over twenty-five years, from banking to my career at Microsoft to my consulting work today, is centered on this strength and passion. In some cases, I was involved from the start, and other times, I got called in to help when things were not going well. In some cases, I would just volunteer or show up at the meetings to help as needed.

Don't fall into the trap of waiting for good things to come to you. There is an old saying: "Good things come to those who wait, but they come a lot faster to those who do something to seek out the good things." Avoid the "If I get promoted, then I can take a class or job shadow someone with the job I want." This kind of thinking stops many people from pursuing their dreams and passions in life.

Take personal steps to grow your self-knowledge and self-mastery, and enjoy the ride now. Even if you don't get the first promotion, you have the chance to learn something along the way and might find a better job later. Don't wait for *someday*. Don't wait until you have all your ducks in a row; start now.

Complete the following exercises. Always strive to be the best you can be at everything you do. Up your game and take proactive steps to increase your self-knowledge and self-mastery and enjoy the process or the ride. My dad always told me two things: one, I can do anything I put my mind to accomplish, and two, don't let anyone tell me I can't.

Personal Leadership Action Plan Part 3—Self-Knowledge and Self-Mastery Application Exercise

Here are some practical tips for gaining both self-knowledge and self-mastery. In the "Stand Up Section," you'll go into more detail on understanding your strengths and how to put them to use to help you become a more effective leader.

1. Make a list of things you enjoy doing at work, at home, or in your volunteer efforts.
2. Make a list of your passions.

3. Find someone you admire who is doing what you want to do, and connect with him or her on LinkedIn or Facebook. Ask him or her for a phone call or meeting to learn what he or she does and what skills are required to be successful in a particular career.

4. Do some research into classes you can take online, at the local community college, or through your work to help you improve.

5. Buy books about your chosen endeavor or check out the books from your local library.

6. Get a subscription to a magazine that talks about your passion.

CHAPTER 9

Leveraging Your Strengths and Being the Best Leader You Can Be

I chose to make my life, my best life!
—Louise Hay

Emotional Intelligence (EQ) Is More Important than IQ

Let's start off this chapter by talking about what makes a great leader. The person's intelligence quotient (IQ) and emotional intelligence (EQ) are two important factors. When it comes to leaders, your EQ, or emotional intelligence, is more important than your IQ. This fact was proven by author Daniel Goldman in his groundbreaking work about emotional intelligence. This is great news for women leaders since women tend to have high EQs.

Daniel Goldman studied thousands of people from young adults to people well into their eighties. He found that people with high EQs were more effective, especially as leaders, than people with very high IQs and low EQs.

The five elements of EQ are the following:

1. Self-awareness—knowing who you are and your strengths and weaknesses
2. Other awareness—understanding how to work with others (especially those who are different from you)
3. Style flexibility—your ability to be flexible and adapt your style

4. Self-motivation—your ability to motivate and keep yourself on course

5. Navigational ability—your ability to navigate change and work in ambiguity

Based on my research and the findings of many other far more qualified researchers than I, women simply seem to do these things better or more naturally. After all, there really is something called women's intuition, and maybe we should learn to listen to it and trust it a little more often.

How often have you been in a situation and something in your heart or stomach tells you there is something rotten in Denmark (which is a silly old saying)? Or on the opposite side, something just feels right? I would be willing to bet for some women, their natural intuition is more often right than wrong.

Know Your Strengths, Find Your Path, and Be True to Yourself

Now, let's talk about finding your strengths, leveraging them, and playing to them every day.

For the past twenty-five years, I've done a lot of work around helping people find their strengths by using various instruments or questionnaires, like the Myers-Briggs Type Indicator (MBTI), DISC profiles, Platinum Rule, Insights, Strength Finder, and many others.

They all have one thing in common; they all started with the groundbreaking work of Dr. Carl Jung from the twenties. Dr. Jung's theory was everyone was born with a set of preferences for how they think, act, and interact with others. Just like some of us are right- or left-hand dominant, we all have a set of preferences for how we make decisions, where we get our energy, how we use our head or heart, how we communicate, and so on.

People can develop *style flexibility*, and do something outside of their strengths, but it will be more difficult, stressful, or just awkward. For example, you could write with your non-dominant or opposite hand, but your handwriting would be terrible and it would feel funny.

I worked with one female leader who was very introverted. She could appear extraverted, but it was physically draining for her to do so. She would schedule the time she needed to go out and greet her employees or customers and then go back to her office to reenergize.

Being extraverted or introverted has little to do with personality; it has to do with where people get their energy. Extraverts get their energy from the outside or being around people and interacting. Introverts get their energy from the inside by reflecting, thinking, and then they are ready to interact or share their ideas.

I love the work of Marcus Buckingham, who has written several books, including, *Now, Go Practice Your Strengths* and *Stand Out.* If you are interested in his work, I encourage you to buy one of his books and take the free assessment that comes with the purchase of the book.

While I am not Marcus Buckingham, I can give you my take on his book and how you apply it to being a strong and successful woman leader. One of Marcus's premises is you need to focus on your strengths and work on improving your strengths over improving your weaknesses.

You improve your weaknesses incrementally. You improve your strengths in quantum leaps. I would rather focus on practicing my strengths any day. To be honest, improving my weaknesses simply drains me.

So how do you determine your strengths?

I mentioned one way is to buy Marcus's book and take the assessment. The other way is to do some reflection on what you do best and what energizes you. You can also ask friends, family, and coworkers what you do best or how they would describe you. There are other personal style instruments, and I'll mention them later in this section, but all the instruments are based on the original works of Dr. Carl Jung and the mother-daughter team of Myers and Briggs.

CHAPTER 10

BIRDS OF A FEATHER FLOCK TOGETHER— SELF-AWARENESS

H ere is a fun way to decide what your strengths are, and it is even more fun to do this with a team or group of people. When I conduct my team-building workshops, I do an exercise to help people determine their strengths and their weaknesses. Many times, I call the workshop "Leveraging Your Strengths and Maintaining Your Peak Performance."

I start off the workshops with an exercise where I ask them to select the one bird that best represents their style of working or thinking or their MO (*modus operandi* in Latin).

The four birds are an eagle, an owl, a peacock, and a dove. See the images below. I'll walk you through this exercise to help you discover your strengths and maintain your peak performance.

Now, select the bird that best represents you and answer the following questions:

1. What words or adjectives describe you?

2. What does your style bring to a team?

3. Pick a motto or song to describe your style?

4. What are the possible downsides of your style? Note—the answer to this one can't be "nothing." ☺

Here is a short summary of each of the styles:

Style/Motto	Characteristics	Strengths	Downsides
Eagle/Red "Be brief, be bold, be gone." Song "We Will Rock You"	direct and to the point, strong and assertive, focused and forceful	gets things done, lets you know where he or she stands, action-oriented	can be seen as aggressive, run over people, can be a poor listener
Peacock/Yellow "Involve and excite me." Song "Celebrate"	lots of passion and energy, positive and assertive, optimistic and fun-loving	brings energy to a team, good sense of humor, people-oriented	can be seen as "flighty," too many ideas, unorganized
Owl/Blue "Give me the details and facts first." Song "Signed, Sealed, and Delivered"	detailed and organized, sees all sides of an issue, thinks before acting	creates order on a team, is structured and calm, task-oriented	analysis paralysis, seen as impersonal, too structured or inflexible
Dove/Green "Show me you care." Song "Feeling"	people oriented, sees the human side, caring and kind	good pulse on people, very good at coaching, brings harmony to the team	can be seen as "soft," delays tough decisions, can hold grudges

One thing to keep in mind is any strength can become a weakness, especially under stress or pressure. Any time someone says you are "too (fill in the blank)," you are at risk of turning a strength into a weakness.

For example, the eagle can move from being assertive and getting things done to being aggressive and pushy. A peacock can move from being positive with a lot of good ideas to being seen as flighty or lacking direction. An owl can move from being detail-oriented and following the rules to suffering from analysis paralysis and being unable to make a decision. And finally, the dove can move from being a caring and kind person to being too soft and unable to make the tough call even when it is the right thing to do.

Style Flexibility and Playing Well with Others

Remember the second part of EQ is "other style awareness and having style flexibility." Now, pick the style that is least like you or hardest for you to work with or understand. Complete these questions:

1. What does this style bring to a team?
2. What do you need to do to work more effectively with this style?

Here is a summary of how to communicate and work with styles or people who are different from you. If you are a leader, adapting your approach to fit the person you are coaching or working with will help you be a better leader for this person.

Style	Dos	Don'ts
Red/Eagles	Get to the point. Be prepared and know your stuff. Speak quickly and directly.	Tell long stories. Wing it or fake it. Get too personal.
Yellow/Peacock	Be excited and upbeat. Speak quickly and with emotion. Focus on new things and ways.	Be overly negative. Be too impersonal. Use a lot of facts.
Blue/Owl	Know your facts. Talk about past and present. Focus on the details.	Get too personal. Dismiss their experience or the past. Be too animated.
Green/Dove	Talk about people issues. Focus on the team. Use their internal radar to get a pulse.	Be too aggressive. Praise publicly. Use too many facts.

There is another instrument or questionnaire similar to Strength Finder called the Platinum Rule by Alessandro Alexander. I like this instrument and his book because is it short and provides some interesting insights.

So, what is the Platinum Rule? We all know what the Golden Rule is, right? The Golden Rule is treat people the way *you* want to be treated.

The Platinum Rule is "treat people the way *they* want to be treated." Strong leaders demonstrate their style flexibility and other awareness by leading people in the right style that suits each individual's needs. Again, this is another area where women tend to do this better than men.

The good thing about the Platinum Rule is you can complete the questionnaire online and get a detailed report on your style strengths, areas for improvement, and how to work with other styles. You can find information on the Platinum Rule at http://www.alessandra.com/abouttony/aboutpr.asp.

I always did a personal style assessment and team-building activity with every team I managed. I found this type of exercise to be invaluable to me as a leader, and it really helped my teams to work together better. I've conducted team-building style exercises using Tinker Toys off-site or even in a bar over cocktails.

CHAPTER 11

LEVERAGE YOUR STRENGTHS AND MAINTAIN YOUR PEAK PERFORMANCE

*My mission in life is not merely to survive, but
to thrive; and to do so with some passion,
some compassion, some humor, and some style!*
—MAYA ANGELOU

Let's face it, we all perform better and stay in our peak performance zone longer when we are working on a job or assignment that plays naturally to our strengths. You perform better, your results are better, and you are happier. You are more motivated when things come naturally to you and you are enjoying the job or the assignment.

My friend Cynthia and I were working on a project for a client on maintaining peak performance and reducing stress. We did a lot of research on the topic and discovered a number of things. One, in any given situation, one person might be in peak performance while the other person is totally stressed out. Two, when people are in a job or role where they can play to their strengths, they are more productive, have less stress, and suffer fewer illnesses that lead to sick days at work.

The other interesting point we discovered and one of the reasons our project was so successful was Cynthia and I are very different people with different styles, different points of view, and different ways of thinking. We've been good friends for thirty-five years, since we worked in banking together. We've remained friends all these years because we both recognize and appreciate our strengths and differences.

One way to focus on a leveraging your strengths is to make a list of the jobs or the types of things that energize you, the things you find yourself doing naturally and enjoy doing. Think outside the box and focus not just on work but the kind of volunteer or community activities you find yourself drawn to all the time. Your strengths are the things that bring you joy and make you feel stronger.

Now, let's look at the opposite side. Think about the kinds of activities that drain you emotionally, mentally, and physically. Think about the things you *have* to do that zap your energy. You avoid or delay doing these things because they actually stress you out. You can do something that is a weaknesses and not your strength, but it is almost painful.

The net-net is a strength makes you feel stronger; you perform better when you are doing it. A weakness is not in your wheelhouse. It literally stresses you out. Don't get me wrong; you can't ignore all your weaknesses, and you can take training classes, read books, or just bite the bullet and do them when you have to, such as under a deadline. But they will never be one of your strengths.

If you go home at the end of the day and feel energized and a true sense of accomplishment, you've probably been spending most of the day in your strength or peak performance zone. If you go home at the end of the day and feel drained or stressed out, you probably spent most of the day in areas where it is hard for you to perform at your best.

For me, my energy zapper is anything to do with detailed paperwork, like filling out expense reports or doing repetitive detail-oriented work. I often got in trouble at the bank for not filling out my expense report when the bank owed me money. I would get a hasty letter from the finance department telling me to fill out my report. If my expense report was more than ninety days late, it had to be signed by the president of the bank.

When I made vice president at the bank, I was invited to a special lunch on the sixtieth floor of the bank's headquarters in downtown Los Angeles. When I met the president of the bank, he said, "Will you please file your expense reports on time? I am tired of signing them." Not a good impression to make on the head honcho!

I've taken a dozen time-management classes and tried various time-management systems. They all work for me for a while, but then I drop most of what I learn and go back to my old way of doing things. So now, I schedule time on my calendar to do my energy-zapping tasks in the morning so I get them over with and start doing things I like, such as creating new solutions to a tough problem no one has been able to solve.

When I was a manager or working on a project, I also surrounded myself with people who had strengths I did not. I remember once working on a project with a woman named Joanne, who was completely the opposite of me. At first, it stressed both of us out, but then we worked out a pattern for our joint projects.

We would meet for a couple of hours and do some brainstorming on the project. We would agree on who would do what on the project, and then we would break apart and perform our individual tasks. We actually worked in a small apartment in West Seattle, and we would go to our separate rooms and do what we did best in our own styles.

She was an introvert and needed time to think, do some research, and reflect. I am an extreme extravert, and I need people to get my energy. We both got what we needed, the projects went very well, and the relationship flourished.

I always tell my kids and groups or individuals I coach about career choices, "Do what you love, and the money will follow."

I saw this on the Internet the other day, and I wanted to pass along these "Ten Rules to Live by."

1. Appreciate what you have before it becomes what you had.
2. Family isn't important; it's everything.
3. Don't pretend to be like everyone else. Don't change to fit in.
4. People inspire you or drain you. Pick wisely.
5. Don't let others dictate your life.
6. It's OK to be scared, but don't let fear stop you.
7. Sometimes silence is better than being right.
8. Avoid overanalyzing. Life is too short to worry about stupid things.
9. Fix it. Deal with it, but stop complaining about it.
10. Sometimes the best you can do is not think, not wonder, not obsess but just breathe and have faith everything will work out for the best.

CHAPTER 12

PERSONAL STYLES AND LEADERSHIP

The future belongs to those who believe
in the beauty of their dreams!
—ELEANOR ROOSEVELT, FORMER FIRST
LADY OF THE UNITED STATES

As I mentioned earlier, having a high EQ is critical to a leader's success. Things like having empathy for others, treating people they way they want to be treated, and being a situational leader are all about EQ. The first two important parts of EQ are understanding and knowing yourself. The second component is understanding others and having style flexibility.

If you are a team leader, leader, or manager, this information is very helpful when it comes to coaching and leading your people. Leadership is situational, meaning how you lead depends to a great degree on who you are leading and their level of skill. If you want to learn about situational leadership, there is a series of books by Ken Blanchard starting with his groundbreaking leadership book entitled *Situational Leadership*.

Imagine for a minute you are a team leader and have been asked to work on a big, important project for your company. You want to assemble the best team, and you know that the best teams are made of people with different skills, experiences, and styles.

You need to select the right team members and get them committed to working on this important project. You have high EQ and great leadership skills and know you need to approach people differently based on their experiences and personal operating styles.

Here is a suggested approach for each team member based on his or her personal operating style.

Style	Your Approach
Red/Eagle	• Be direct and to the point. • Talk about how important and visible the project is to upper management. • Talk fast and be prepared. • Avoid giving a lot of details. • Avoid small talk and chitchat.
Yellow/Peacock	• Be upbeat, enthusiastic, and faster paced. • Talk quickly and brainstorm for a few ideas. • Talk about how the project is a chance to make a difference. • Stress the project focuses on new ways of doing things and innovation. • Avoid excessive details and long history lessons on the project.
Blue/Owl	• Be factual and describe the details. • Slow down your pace of speech. • Talk about the background or history of the project. • Discuss the past, present, and future (how things fit together). • Honor his or her experience and organizational skills. • Avoid small talk and personal chitchat.
Green/Dove	• Be caring and respectful. • Slow down your pace of speech. • Focus on the people issues. • Talk about how the project will help employees and customers. • Tell them you need them to be the glue that holds the team together. • Don't be too assertive or aggressive.

I always have a "So what?" point or slide in my workshops, webinars, and speeches. So what does knowing my strengths do to help me become a better leader?

Working in your strength zone will help you be a better leader, team member, or person by doing the following:

1. Boosting your personal productivity
2. Improving your team, customer, and personal relationships

3. Achieving your best and maximizing your impact
4. Building your team and leadership skills
5. Reducing your stress

Working in your strength zone at work and in your personal life will make your life better.

CHAPTER 13

Change Is Hard and Takes Practice, Patience, and Persistence

Champions have the courage to keep turning the pages
because they know a better chapter lies ahead!
—Paula White

A s you read this book or try to make any changes in your life, you need to realize that change is hard and takes a combination of practice, patience, and persistence. A lot of people say practice makes perfect. I say practice makes permanent. In order to change, whether you are trying to lose weight, quit smoking, or stop biting your nails, it takes time, and you need to be conscious of your actions.

I mentioned earlier in my book my good friend and fellow author Laura Steward wrote a great book called *What would a Wise Woman Do?* The wonderful thing about Laura's book is she shows the power of using questions to guide you through life.

Here are some questions to consider in regards to the changes you need to make to become the kind of leader and person you want to be. Ask yourself if what you are doing or planning on doing is consistent with your vision and values. Ask your yourself, "Is what I am doing going to help me to become the person and leader I want to be or prevent me from getting there?"

There is an old saying that the only person who likes change is a baby with a dirty diaper. You need to feed your mind with positive thoughts and actions. What you tell yourself dictates the programs that are recorded in your brain. To make change stick, you have to behave the way you want to be. Here is a diagram that shows the connection between what you think and how you behave.

For example, an event or something happens in a meeting that is very stressful for you. Your mind goes through a fairly predictable process in nanoseconds. The event triggers a set of your beliefs (good or bad) based on past experience. Very quickly, your mind filters this event through your values, which triggers your action or reaction. When you *react*, you are acting without thinking.

You and only you control how you think, act, or respond, so you can choose to respond differently. For example, rather than getting upset in the meeting, you could choose to let it go since the issue is not that important to you. You could choose to say something in the meeting and express your opinion. You can choose to change, period.

Here is one of my favorite quotes from Mahatma Gandhi:

> Your beliefs become your thoughts,
> Your thoughts become your words,
> Your words become your actions,
> Your actions become your habits,
> Your habits become your values,
> Your values become your destiny.
> —MAHATMA GANDHI

Focus on What You Can Control

Stephen Covey, the famous author, came out with a series of books starting with the very popular *Seven Habits of Highly Successful People*. Each book in this series outlines the critical habits that made one person more effective than the others of average performance.

One of the concepts I really liked and fits here when it comes to change and forgiving yourself and others is the "Circle of Influence." Here is what the circle looks like.

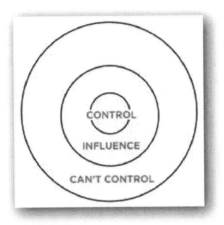

The center of the circle represents your circle of control. The only thing you can control on the planet is yourself. You can control how you think, feel, act, and respond. You can control whether a situation is stressful for you or drives you to peak performance.

As much as you may try, you can't control your kids, your husband, your boss, or the people you lead. As a parent, you can provide your kids a good set of beliefs and guidance as they grow up, but you can't control them. You can try to change your husband, wife, or significant other, but unless he or she chooses to change, he or she won't because you cannot control him or her either.

The second circle is the circle of influence, and this is where the magic and your power lie. You can either expand or make your circle of influence smaller, depending on how you think, feel, act, and behave.

Your circle of influence expands when you choose to act in a positive manner and influence other people in a positive way.

Your circle of influence starts to become smaller when you think, act, feel, or respond in a negative manner. Your circle of influence shrinks when you do things like participate in gossip about other people. Your circle of influence gets smaller when you are always negative and have nothing positive to say or do.

The final outside circle is your circle of concern, or the things you can't control. These are things you may be genuinely concerned about, but you can't control or influence them. You can't control the economy, the current weather, and even things like company reorganizations, which seemed to happen a lot in the two industries I worked in.

Spending time in this outer circle can set some people off spinning, or participating in what I call "awfulizing." Saying things like "Isn't this the economy awful?" or "Isn't this reorganization awful for us?" is not productive and usually only makes the situation worse. People can dwell on the things they can't control, and they in turn reduce the size of their circle of influence and their ability to have a positive impact on others.

I remember one time when I worked in banking and we were reorganizing the company again, which seemed to happen on an annual or regular basis. I was "awfulizing" to my boss, Larry, who said, "You can't control whether the bank choses to reorganize again, and spending time worrying about it will only stress you out. Stop worrying about what-ifs. Concentrate your energy on doing the best you can, keep your eyes open for new opportunities, and when the reorganization is over, simply pick up your briefcase and move on to your next adventure."

Wise words to live by, indeed. Later in my career when I worked at Microsoft, I remembered what Larry said and made a choice to focus on what I could control and try to influence things as best I could by stating my opinion on the reorganization, but I no longer lay awake at night "awfulizing" about the frequent reorganizations.

Keep this model of the circle of control, influence, and concern in mind as you read this book and, more important, as you go through life.

Personal and Leadership Action Plan Part 4
Leverage Your Strengths Action Steps

1. Make a list of all of your strengths and the things you do naturally.
2. Make a list of things you love or enjoy doing.
3. Make a list of the things you hate doing or find personally draining.
4. For two weeks, keep a personal energy journal. Write down what time you wake, what time you go to bed, and when you feel most energized during the day or night.
5. You have three choices after you complete this exercise:
   a. You can talk to your manager and team about how to incorporate your strengths into your existing job.
   b. You can start the process of finding a new job (sometimes in the same company) where you can play to your strengths.
   c. You can find ways to exercise your strengths and skills outside of work to keep yourself energized and find a better job that fits your strengths later.
6. Here are some tips to leverage and play to your strengths:
   a. Buy the book *Strength Finder* by Marcus Buckingham and take the free assessment that comes with the purchase of the book. I get nothing for promoting Marcus's work, but I've loved his work and approach for years.
   b. Buy the book *The Platinum Rule* by Alessandro Alexander and take the questionnaire to figure out your style.
   c. Practice leveraging your strengths every day.
   d. If you are working, go to your boss and ask if you can work on special projects that fit your strengths.
   e. If you are in a job that you need financially but doesn't offer more projects that fit your strengths, do volunteer work that plays to your strengths. You'll be playing to your strengths and helping with a good cause.
   f. Find people around you or build a team with people who are different from you.
   g. If you are a leader, build your team with people with different styles to ensure your team is balanced.

SECTION 3

STAND UP

You can be amazing
You can turn a phrase into a weapon or a drug
You can be the outcast
Or be the backlash of somebody's lack of love
Or you can start speaking up.
Nothing's gonna hurt you the way that words do
When they settle 'neath your skin
Kept on the inside and no sunlight
Sometimes a shadow wins
But I wonder what would happen if you

Say what you wanna say
And let the words fall out
Honestly I wanna see you be brave
—SARA BAREILLES, "BRAVE"

CHAPTER 14

CATHY'S STORY

You may stumble and fall and yet you rise up!
—MAYA ANGELOU

Cathy started out like many young girls; she was smart and very good in math and science. She excelled in both subjects from elementary school through high school. When she graduated, she decided to go to college and major in engineering, following in her father's footsteps. Cathy continued to excel at college and graduated with honors after four years.

Upon graduation, Cathy landed a well-paying job with a top engineering firm about an hour from her house. Cathy thrived at work and was promoted up the ranks of management until she was a senior manager of one of the largest technical departments at the firm.

After about six years with the firm, Cathy and her husband decided it was time to have kids. When Cathy told her boss excitedly that she was pregnant, he was less than pleased. He said he could not afford to lose Cathy at this time since they were involved in one of the biggest projects in the company's history and he needed Cathy to head up the team.

Cathy agreed she would head up the team until two weeks before her due date but said that she would leave for her six weeks of leave at that point. She promised to return to work after her six weeks of maternity leave.

Cathy returned to work as promised, but when she returned to work, her priorities shifted. She still worked hard but left work every day at six to pick up her daughter and head home for dinner. Cathy's husband pitched in when he could with the baby and with the housework since they both had demanding full-time jobs.

After about six months of trying to balance a highly demanding job and a new family, Cathy realized she no longer was in love with the job. The job started requiring her to travel overnight a couple times a month, which meant she had to leave her baby with her husband or mother overnight.

The stress of the job, the overnight travel, and being a mother and wife was wearing on Cathy. She started to read a lot about finding her strengths so she could decide where she best fit. She knew she needed to move to a new role within her current company or go to work someplace else.

Cathy finally went to her manager for help. Luckily, her manager understood Cathy's dilemma and agreed to help her in any he could so she could stay at the company and be happy. Her manager checked around with a couple of his peers and it turns out there was a job in another department that would fit Cathy's strengths and talents.

Cathy moved to the marketing department and continued to thrive. The role fit her strengths perfectly and did not require overnight travel or long hours. Cathy was good at engineering, but she loved the creativity side of the business in marketing.

After a few years, her daughter was in school, and Cathy was promoted to be the general manager of the marketing department, where she continued to thrive for many years. When I asked her if she wanted to become vice president of marketing or some other higher role, she said no. Cathy said she was perfectly happy with her role as GM because she got to lead a great team of marketing professionals and could go home to her family at a reasonable hour.

When I asked Cathy what she learned from this experience, she explained a number of things. First Cathy learned that it is OK to put your career aside to take care of something more important to you, like having a family, caring for an aging parent, or going back to school.

She also learned that it is important to play to your strengths and find a job that fits you. Cathy confessed that even though she thrived in the first role, she felt like a square peg in a round hole. She took the job to please her dad and become an engineer just like him, but the job never felt right to her.

In Cathy's view, the entire experience made her a better leader. She could empathize with her people more and understand where they were coming from. As a leader, Cathy made a point of understanding her people and their strengths. She tried to make sure her team members were in the right roles, roles that fit them, played to their strengths, and allowed them to soar.

Newsflash—Female Leaders Are More Engaging than Male Leaders

Wow, here is some new and interesting research from the Gallup Company. Most people know or recognize the name Gallup from the political or TV surveys they conduct, but Gallup has a large research base on employee engagement, leadership, customer-centricity, and so on.

In their recent study, Gallup found the following to be true of female leaders:

1. Only one in three working Americans say they have a female boss.
2. Female leaders are more engaged than their male counterparts.
3. Companies need to hire and promote more female leaders.

In 1953, when Gallup ran a survey and asked working Americans if they preferred to work for a man or a woman, at the time, two-thirds of the people surveyed preferred a male leader, 5 percent said they preferred a female leader, and 25 percent said it did not matter.

Fast-forward to today and the differences are amazing. Today, one-third of working Americans prefer a male, 20 percent said they prefer a woman, and 46 percent said it did not matter.

The even more interesting fact from Gallup's *State of American Managers Analytics and Advice for Leader's Report* was that employees who worked for a female leader were more engaged on average than those who worked for a male leader. Hooray!

In addition, female leaders themselves are more engaged than their male counterparts: 41 percent of the female leaders are more engaged at work as compared to their male counterparts at 35 percent. In fact, female leaders are more engaged in every age group or generation whether they had children or not. If female leaders are more engaged, it seems to be reasonable to think that female leaders bring more passion to the workplace and contribute more to the organization's results.

Higher Level of Engagement Means Higher Productivity and Better Business Results

When I teach my leadership workshops, I often talk about the three "P's" of business performance. How you treat your *people* impacts how they *perform* with your customers which directly impacts your *profitability*.

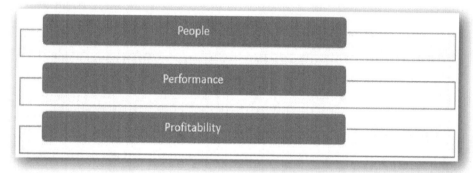

It always surprises me when some people don't see the connection between how leaders treat their people and the bottom line. To me, it simply seems logical.

It is like a circle. If leaders treat their people well and meet their needs, their performances are better and they are more engaged. People who are more engaged deliver better customer service. If you're treating your people well, you'll have less turnover. If you have happy employees and happy customers, you have fewer customer complaints. If you have happy customers, you have higher customer retention, which finally leads to higher profitability. Of course, the opposite is true too. The chart above illustrates this point.

Given that female leaders are more engaged than male leaders, it simply seems logical that the female leaders' workgroups or teams are more engaged and therefore more productive. Gallup's research points out the employees who work for a female leader are six percentage points more engaged than the employees who work for male leaders.

There is an old saying "A picture is worth a thousand words." Well, the following chart tells it all:

FEMALE MANAGERS ARE BETTER AT ENGAGING THEIR EMPLOYEES THAN MALE MANAGERS

Employees who work for a female manager are more engaged, on average, than those who work for a male manager, according to a Gallup study of U.S. employees. Women who report to female managers have the highest engagement, while men who report to male managers have the lowest engagement.

Percentage of employees engaged

25% — Male Manager Male Employee
29% — Female Manager Male Employee
31% — Male Manager Female Employee
35% — Female Manager Female Employee

GALLUP

The research also suggests female leaders are more caring and take a stronger interest in the development of their people than male leaders do. Female leaders are more likely to promote their employees based on their potential to succeed in a new role. Female leaders are also more likely to find job assignments and challenges for employees to help them grow.

These facts about female leaders being more engaged, caring, and involved in their employees' performance are very important for the millennials joining today's workplace. I read an article by one of Gallup's consultants that money is important to millennials, but engaged millennials are less likely to leave over money.

While some of these findings may be hard for some people to swallow, the impact is clear. Organizations should focus on hiring, promoting, and developing more female leaders across the board.

CHAPTER 15

BEING A GREAT LEADER AND COACH

> *No matter what you're going through, there's a light*
> *at the end of the tunnel and it may seem hard to get*
> *to it but you can do it and just keep working toward*
> *it and you'll find the positive side of things!*
> —DEMI LOVATO

As I mentioned earlier in the book, in today's constantly changing, permanent whitewater environment, we need more leaders or coaches and fewer managers or directors. One of the classic differences cited in a lot of leadership books is that managers seem to direct and tell, while leaders empower and ask insightful and thought-provoking questions.

I was told many years ago that people believe what they discover for themselves more than when someone tells them what to do and how to do it. To me, a leader who understands the power of using questions to help people discover for themselves is more effective than a manager who tells people how to do things.

One of the key differentiators of strong female leaders over strong male leaders is that women tend to be better or more natural developers of people. As female leaders, we need to take this natural talent and use it to our advantage.

So, how do you become a better leader or coach?

One, you ask more questions. Two you coach with *CARE*.

Many years ago, when I was developing a new course for a client on how to coach people, I needed a simple model or way to communicate to my learners how to coach. I know this might seem silly, but I came up with my Coaching with CARE model for my workshop called Coaching for Business Results.

The model is simple and easy to remember and follow. It involves four simple steps, which reinforce the power of questions. The coaching with CARE model is as follows:

1. Connect—connect with people based on their personal style
2. Access—access or ask people questions about their point of view
3. Reinforce—reinforce your point of view or what you need them to do
4. Establish—establish an action or improvement plan

Simple, right? This simple model can be adapted to your style and the styles of the people you are leading. And it works very well since you are starting by asking questions and hearing their point of view before you reinforce your expectations of their performance. Finally, you develop a quick action plan or improvement plan to get people back on track.

I encourage you to give this a try the next time you need to coach someone. Before any coaching session, I always write out the questions I want to ask beforehand. A wise leader I worked for many years ago told me, "If the only sound you hear in a coaching session is your own voice, you are talking to yourself."

The other challenging point with some more traditional management or coaching models is that when you tell people what to do and how to do it, they don't own the problem or the solution. You own it. Their commitment level will be much higher if they own the problem and solution.

So my call to the female leaders reading this book is "Let's go kick some glass!"

So how do you become the kind of leader you want to be? Where do you start to become a high-performing leader people want to follow? You start by writing your personal leadership vision.

CHAPTER 16

DEVELOP YOUR PERSONAL AND PROFESSIONAL VISION—YOU INC.

> *I love to see a young girl go out and grab the world by the lapels. Life's a bitch. You've got to go out and kick ass!*
> —MAYA ANGELOU

S o, what are the components that go into your personal brand and You Inc.? There are five key components of your personal brand shown in the following illustration.

Throughout this book, you'll be building your brand and your new company, You Inc. We'll start off in this section with your vision and values. The next section will cover discovering your strengths and talents. And finally, this entire book is about building on your past experiences and taking your performance to the next level to become the leader you want to be.

Nations have visions, companies have visions, and every leader should have a personal leadership vision to guide and help her become the leader she wants to be. Think of your vision as You Inc. and your personal brand.

In order to *stand up*, you need to have a deep understanding of what you are standing up for and you need solid ground to stand up on. You need something to help you stay centered and focused on who you are and what kind of person or leader you want to be. You need a vision that stands the test of time and sets you apart from others.

Each woman needs to think about her identity as a leader, choose what she wants, and work toward creating her desired identity intentionally. Work with a purpose and a passion to propel your success to whatever level you choose. The power of your vision needs to be personal to you and your voice.

Here is a short story to illustrate a vision.

Someone walked by Michelangelo when he was sculpting the famous statue of David and asked him, "How do you take a huge slab of stone and turn it into a work of art and statue like the perfect image of David?"

Michelangelo looked up and responded, "I looked into the stone and saw my vision of David, and I simply take away everything that is not David."

The same technique can be used in life; we simply need to take out everything that is no longer needed, helpful, or necessary. We do not need to create who we are; we were born perfect and created perfect with everything we needed to be successful. We need to simply take away everything that is not us or does not help us grow stronger.

We need to discover who we are and what makes us stronger and let go of everything else. Think about this question: Who am I? Asking this question throughout your life with sincerity and consistency can help you be strong despite the many roadblocks you face. It will help you discover who you are and what is important to you.

One of the most important things you can do is realize who you really are, what you stand for, and what is really important to you. You are not your name, which might change. You are more than a daughter, sister, or mom because your identity goes beyond the roles you play. You are not your job because most people have several different jobs in their lives. You are not your bank account, which might rise or fall in your lifetime.

Most companies have a vision, mission, and a set of operating principles or values they use to ensure the company continues to grow and stay focused on who they are. They hire staff or consultants to help create their vision and establish a brand, which represents the image they want to project to the world to help them be successful.

When I experienced my fall from the top of the mountain, one of the most powerful things that happened was I realized I had stopped living my vision and walking my values. I had completely lost my sense of who I was and what I stood for, and I was lost in a pile of work and exhaustion. One of the things that pulled me back up the mountain was reviving my personal vision and values.

Do you have a personal or professional vision you use to guide you, help you make tough decisions, and keep you centered?

One of the things that can keep you centered, help guide you through all the changes in the world, and serve as a road map on your journey is your personal vision. So, let's start with some background on what a vision is, where it comes from, and how to use a personal vision to be the kind of leader you want to be.

Vision—Background and History

> *Vision without action is a dream...*
> *Action without vision merely passes the time...*
> *Action with vision can change the world.*
> —JOEL BARKER, *THE POWER OF VISION*

So where did the concept of vision come from and why is it so important when leading today? To satisfy my strange habit of wanting to figure out where things came from, I started doing research into *vision*, its history, and how to use a powerful and compelling vision to provide clarity of action in this turbulent world.

Famous author and business guru Joel Barker conducted extensive research into the origin of the concept of vision, which has become very popular in business over the last twenty years. The first reference to the power of vision came from the Dutch scholar Fred Pollack, who wrote a book called *The Image of the Future.*

What Pollack found when he studied nations going back to ancient Greece and Rome was all successful nations had one thing in common. They all had a powerful and compelling vision that led to their success. When you look at nations like Greece, Rome, Britain, Spain, and United States, you can see they all had a vision of the future that was better than what currently existed.

Many of these nations did not start out strong and powerful, and in many cases, they did not have the right resources to be successful, but they did have a vision. Pollard said, "Nations with visions are powerful... Nations without visions are at risk."

According to Joel Barker's research, which he presents in his book and video *The Power of Vision,* another example of vision dates back to World War II with some research into why some people survived the Nazi concentration camps and other people died. The book by Victor Frankel called *Man's Search for Meaning* described Victor's time in the concentration camps as a young doctor.

Victor Frankel was a successful doctor in Vienna, but he was also Jewish. He was rounded up like all the other Jews and shipped off to a place that was truly a living hell.

Victor Frankel had three goals during his time in the concentration camp:

1. to survive
2. to use his medical skills to help others
3. to learn something

Two men were about to commit suicide since dying was better than living for them. Victor wanted to help the men survive and learn something. He talked to the men and helped them discover that they had something left to live for after the concentration camp. One man had a child who was waiting for him. The other man was a scientist and had a project that only he could complete. The two men did not commit suicide and went on to live after the camp.

Frankel tells his story so well. "Almost in tears and in pain, I kept thinking of the endless trivial problems daily and hourly things I had to do to survive the moment. Should I have traded my last cigarette for a piece of bread? How could I find a piece of wire to use as a shoelace? I forced my thoughts to the future and where I wanted to be. A place that was significantly better than my current horrible environment. I closed my eyes and imagined I was standing on stage in a large, warm, and pleasant lecture room by a podium. I imagined myself giving a speech to an eager audience in comfortable chairs sharing what I learned in the concentration camp."

The one thing the survivors had in common was they all had a very clear vision of something that kept them alive despite the terrible conditions in which they were living for many years. The survivors all had something important in their minds to live for beyond the walls of the concentration camp. One man had an image of his daughter picking flowers every day. One woman wanted to write a book to help women become better mothers. They all had something to live for, something important to do, and a clear image in their minds of something that was fundamentally better than their current circumstances.

So what did Victor Frankel learn by studying the survivors of the concentration camps? He discovered that "all those who survived had something significant left to do in the future."

More Recent Examples of Vision

The concept of vision became popular in sports with skier Jean Claude Kelley during the Winter Olympics in 1968. Sportswriters and fans would watch Jean Claude stand at the top of the mountain going through his trip down the mountain to win the gold medal in his mind. He would stand at the top of the mountain and see an image or vision of himself going through every turn and down every hill. He would move his body before he ever started down the mountain and raise his hands in victory as he went through the imaginary finish line.

Mary Kay Ash, founder of Mary Kay Cosmetics, had an amazing vision when she founded her company in 1963. Her company is the sixth largest sales organization in the world. Mary Kay's original vision since she founded the company has been "to give women the opportunity to be the best they could be and succeed at everything they do."

Classic business and visionary leaders have developed strong and powerful visions for their companies, which helped them unite everyone in the company or charitable organization, helped them stay focused, and helped them make tough decisions. Walt Disney's vision was to create "the happiest place on earth where everyone can feel like a kid again." Steve Jobs and Steve Wozniak's vision for Apple was "to change the way the world works." The vision for Microsoft by Bill Gates and Paul Allen was "to have a computer on every desk and in every home." Both companies achieved their visions when at the time, they were not the largest companies and did not have the most employees or the highest revenue.

Businesses, nonprofit organizations, sports leaders, and prisoners of war use these powerful visions to help guide them, to stay centered, to be true to who they are, and to help them make the right decisions, especially when things get tough.

So what is a vision and how can it help you to stand up? In *Alice in Wonderland*, when Alice was lost, she asked the Cheshire cat which way to go. The cat looked down, smiled, and said, "If you don't know where you are going, any path will get you there."

A vision is a signpost on your journey in life. It is a road map that gets you from point A to point B. It is a compass that tells you whether you are headed in the right direction. I use my personal and leadership vision to help me make career and life choices.

Every time I made a decision to take a job or project that was aligned with my vision, I soared and I loved the work. Every time I made a decision to take a job or project that was not aligned with my vision, it was the project or job from hell. I've taken a number of lateral career moves to get an experience to help broaden my strengths, consistent with my vision.

There is some confusion in the business world and among business authors on the true definition of things like *mission, vision,* and *values.* Let me try to simplify and clarify these terms.

- A mission is what you do.
- A vision is a statement of where you want to be.
- Values determine how you will act, behave, and treat others and allow you to live your vision and achieve your mission.

Let me provide an example. When I went to Microsoft in 1998, our mission was to develop the best software on the plant. Our vision was to live in a world where there was a computer on every desk and in every home around the globe. A few of our values were the following:

- passion for technology and people
- treating people with respect and dignity
- honoring our commitments
- taking on big challenges

Over time, the mission, vision, and values were modified to fit the current competitive environment, but the foundation has stayed fairly consistent.

I've had a personal and professional vision, which I developed while attending a training session over twenty-five years ago. My vision is to *make a difference and empower people to achieve their full potential.* I use my personal vision to define who I work for, the kinds of jobs and projects I choose to work on, what I stand for, and how to make the right decision in order to stay true to who I am and what I believe.

Some of my person values are the following:

- Treat everyone with respect and dignity regardless of who they are and what they do.
- Treat everyone the way they want to be treated.
- Help people grow and be the best they can be.
- Be passionate in everything you do.
- Live my vision. Walk my values.
- Have fun.

Let me give a quick example of how I put my values to work. One of my favorite jobs at Microsoft was running a new-hire program called MS 101. We flew ninety newly hired sales and service people from around the world to be at the Microsoft corporate headquarters in Redmond, Washington, for a week.

For an entire week, we gave them an overview of the company. They met many of our top executives and toured places like the Microsoft Home of the Future and our Executive Briefing Center (EBC). The first night, we hosted all ninety new hires, who many times were from twenty-five to thirty different counties at a special dinner with our executives at the EBC.

At one point, I overheard a young lady yelling at one of the receptionists to get her a taxi now. This lady had graduated with an MBA from one of the nation's top schools. She was telling this receptionist she was a nobody and she could jump up and help her.

I walked over and asked the young lady to step aside to a private area to talk. I said her actions were completely inappropriate. I told her if I ever heard her to talk to any employee in the same manner, I would report her to her manager. I told her to go apologize to the receptionist and please go back to the hotel. She had violated one of my top values, and I took action.

The times in my life when I did not use my vision to make the right choice when faced with a tough decision, I regretted the decision and was miserable in the end. When I was going through my fall a couple of years ago, I had been ignoring my vision for some time and taking jobs or projects that, in my heart, I knew were not aligned with my vision.

A lot of companies take the time to have the executives go off to some off-site retreat to develop the company's vision and values. Many times, the executives come back from their retreat and share their visions with the rest of the company. There is usually a lot of hoopla and ceremony around the newly formed vision and values.

Some companies give out T-shirts, stickers and wallet cards and paste the vision and their values on the walls of the office. All of this is fine, but the problem is in many companies, everything stops there. A few years later, someone comes into the office and says something about the vision and values and an employee says, "Oh, that was something the executives developed at some off-site, but nobody really uses this."

A vision is only valuable and useful if you use it to guide and direct what you do as an organization or as a leader. A vision and values are useful to help you make tough decisions when faced with two or more alternatives. When faced with this tough decision, ask yourself which of the alternatives is more aligned with your vision.

Live your vision…Leave a legacy!

I Stumbled, but I Did Not Fall

I know the techniques I recommend you try in this book work because I've used things like maximizing my strengths and having a personal vision to guide me and they worked for me many times.

I talked about my fall earlier in the book and how I managed to pull myself up from the bottom of the mountain and start to climb up again. After about a year, I slowly started to feel better and get my confidence back, but if I was being honest with myself, I would have had to admit I was not there yet.

At my lowest point during my fall, I would rate my energy, my happiness, and my ability to do things a three to five on a ten-point scale with one being low and ten being the best. After I applied the concepts recommended by my doctors and coach, I managed to climb to a six on most days and sometimes as high as a seven on a really good day.

However, I was still experiencing things like not being able to lose weight no matter how little I ate or how much I exercised. I still felt like I had foggy brain and low energy and could not think clearly. I was still losing my hair, and to be honest, my self-esteem and self-confidence were pretty low. I could not sleep and usually woke up four to five times a night.

My husband saw an ad in the newspaper describing every one of my symptoms to a T. It was for an integrated medical group that promised a natural way to cure things like hypothyroidism, diabetes, and all my problems.

I decided to call the clinic and went to my first appointment with my husband. It was a requirement of the clinic that the spouse attend the first appointment. They ran a series of tests, including one for my cortisol levels, a lot of blood tests, and even a stool test. Yes, I had to poop in a little dish, put it in a plastic bag, and ship it to a lab for someone to examine. Major yuck!

When the tests came back, it turned out I had something called Hashimoto's, which is an autoimmune disease related to the thyroid. The thyroid is a small butterfly-shaped organ in your neck that controls a lot of functions in the body.

When I told a friend I had Hashimoto's disease, the response was, "I did not know you were Japanese." Hashimoto's disease was discovered by Dr. Hashimoto and is similar to other autoimmune diseases, like Lupus and Graves' disease.

I went on a strict diet for thirty days to determine my allergy sensitivities or possible allergies and a number of natural medicines and supplements. It turns out I had food sensitivities to a number of things like dairy, soy, gluten, and a few other things. The main difference between a food allergy and a food sensitivity is many times when someone is an allergic to a food, he or she has very severe reactions, like swelling of the tongue or mouth and possible death in some cases.

A food sensitivity is where you can eat the food and not experience a severe reaction, but your body does not digest it well and usually results in something like feeling sluggish, bloated, and the other things I was experiencing.

I followed the program for six months, lost the thirty-five pounds I had gained, and started to feel great again. I also jump-started my personal program of taking care of myself, doing my morning routine, and started reading things I enjoyed. I soon began to feel like nine or ten most days.

After all the doctors and nurses telling me I had chronic fatigue, extreme stress, and depression, I found out I had an autoimmune disease that could be treated without potentially dangerous depression medication and sleeping pills.

The tipping point for me was in church on Easter Sunday, I started writing that day and have not stopped. In fact, I've already started on a second book.

My business suddenly started to move in the right direction. I attended business networking events and met people. This time, I followed up with people I had something in common with or who might have a need for my leadership and consulting services.

My creativity came back too. When I was at the bottom of the mountain, I tried to be creative and motivated, but there was nothing there. I had writer's block and a creativity brain fart. I started to design and write new leadership and team workshops. I started to volunteer and make a difference with a number of groups in my area.

I started speaking at business networking groups, including an executive group that meets once a month in Orange County. I started attending and speaking at women's events, like Women in Technology and Lean In. I worked on my marketing materials and developing my Speaker One sheet.

As I write this book, I have booked a number of radio show interviews and I hope to be on a show like *Ellen* or a morning show like *Good Morning America* or the *Today Show*. Wish me luck!

Personal Leadership Vision Application Exercise Part 5

Here are some practical tips for developing your personal and leadership vision.

1. Take out a piece of paper. Find your favorite quiet or peaceful place.
2. Imagine your favorite magazine is going to write an article about you as a person and you as a leader.
3. Write down the words, adjectives, or thoughts that come to mind when you complete this sentence:

   [Insert your name] is the premier example of a great world-class leader, and he or she embodies the essence of leadership. Here is a list of the leadership characteristics he or she exhibits on a daily basis...

4. Fine-tune your vision and get it down to a short sentence you could print on a business card or say in ten seconds or less.
5. Use your personal and leadership vision to make decisions about your career and your life and when faced with a tough choice between two or more options. For example, ask yourself, "Which of these two choices will get me closer to living my personal vision and being my true self?"
6. Develop your own personal values. Use your values to make sure you stay the course and do the right things.

7. To develop your coaching skills, you can do any of the following:
   a. Take a free coaching class online.
   b. Enroll in a coaching class at a local college or university.
   c. Take a workshop through your work if they offer training classes on coaching.
   d. Practice your coaching skills in your day-to-day interactions with your team.

SECTION 4
STAND OUT

It's time for me to take it
I'm the boss right now
Not gonna fake it
Not when you go down
'Cause this is my game
And you better come to play

I used to hold my freak back
Now I'm letting go
I make my own choice
Bitch, I run this show
So leave the lights on

No, you can't make me behave
So you say I'm complicated
That I must be outta my mind
But you had me underrated
Rated, rated

What's wrong with being, what's wrong with being confident?

—Demi Lovato, "Confident"

CHAPTER 17

BUILDING YOUR SELF-CONFIDENCE

You can't give away what you do not own!
—BOBBIE GEE

Joan's Story—Standing Out above the Crowd

Joan thrived as a senior administrative executive in various health-care environments over her thirty-year career.

One of Joan's challenges was overcoming the opinions most physicians had of the administration function and those who worked as administrators, especially women.

One night, after a hospital charity event, the chief of surgery physically cornered her in his office until she was able to break free.

Confused and humiliated, she reported the incident to human resources according to hospital policy. Human resources told her there was nothing she could do, as his prominence in his field as well the revenue he brought in was too important to the hospital's overall reputation.

As a single mom, Joan needed the job to support her family. The incident and lack of support from the organization weighed on her, and she could feel her self-confidence begin to dwindle. The offending doctor began to speak ill of her with colleagues and put her down in front of patients and staff. She started doubting herself on a regular basis in all aspects of her life. She found herself pulling away from the things she loved to do like read, sew, travel, and volunteer in the community.

After about a year, a friend of Joan's pulled her aside to find out what was going on with her. Joan told her what had happened, and they both cried. Her friend told Joan she had had a similar experience at work. The two of them made a pact to help each other out in the future.

They started meeting for lunch once a week and formed their own "book club." They read a number of self-help books and decided to put a few of the techniques to work. They went to the store together to buy a gratitude journal and a special beautiful bond notebook to write their personal affirmations.

Joan confessed to her friend that she felt silly at first talking to the mirror in her bathroom and saying her positive affirmations, but after a week or so, she found she enjoyed it. Joan's favorite place to do her affirmations was in her car on the way to and from work.

Slowly, Joan's confidence came back, and she felt better about herself. She started to pick up her old hobbies, like reading and sewing and even took up quilting. She made a pact with herself to always to put herself first on her priority list.

Here are the three things Joan learned from her experience:

1. Never to let someone else define her and her self-worth
2. Take responsibility for her life and live her life by her rules and not the rules of others
3. Always stay focused on and live your values every day

Eventually Joan left the hospital and found a great job with a very large health-care provider in the Pacific Northwest, which was closer to her family. Joan mentors a number of women and volunteers at her daughter's school, teaching young girls self-esteem and how to have confidence.

Joan founded a women's leadership group for women to share their successes and challenges and help each other. Interestingly, five years later, the harassing doctor was fired after several women reported similar experiences.

CHAPTER 18

WHAT'S WRONG WITH BEING CONFIDENT?

A woman with a voice is by definition a strong woman. But the search to find that voice can be remarkably difficult.
—MELINDA GATES

As Demi Lovato sings in her song, "What's wrong with being confident?"

So, what is self-confidence? Back to my strange habit of trying to figure out the meaning of words and finding the root or origin of the word. When you look up the word *self-confidence* in the good old *Webster's Dictionary*, it offers the following: "the state of mind characterized by one's reliance on oneself or a feeling of self-sufficiency, a feeling or belief that you can do something well or succeed at something, a feeling or belief that someone or something is good or has the ability to succeed at something."

The problem is sometimes when a woman is confident, people see her as bossy or bitchy. There was a campaign last year during Women's History Month to ban the word *bossy* since it is more often used to refer to women than men. I was surprised by the amount of negative press about this campaign. The TV ads featured a lot of famous women like Beyoncé, Halle Berry, Sheryl Sandberg, and many other famous women saying, "We need to ban the word *bossy*," and some people were offended by the campaign.

The sad fact is women who come across as too confident are sometimes seen as bossy and sometimes bitchy. Sheryl Sandberg, in her book

Lean In, cites a classic Harvard Business School study where a group of students were given two case studies to read and analyze. One was about a male manager named Howard, and the other was about a female leader named Heidi.

All the facts in the two cases were exactly the same. The students who read about Howard said he was a leader, strategic thinker, strong, assertive, and effective. The students who read about Heidi described her as bossy, aggressive, not a team player, and pushy. Even though the facts were exactly the same and the only difference was the name of the leader in the story, the students viewed the woman's performance negatively.

A second more visual example, which you can find on YouTube, is a Pantene shampoo commercial from the Philippines. I show this video in my training classes and webinars. The commercial shows a young woman getting ready to go to work, and the word that pops up is *vain*. The next scene shows a man getting ready, and the word that pops up is *neat*. The next scene shows the woman standing up in a meeting, and the word that pops up is *aggressive*. The next scene shows a man standing up in a meeting, and the word is *assertive*. And so on.

There is a fine line between being assertive and being aggressive. To be honest, there have been times in my life when I've been told I am too aggressive and I try to watch myself and prevent myself from crossing the line.

I went back to my faithful dictionary and looked up "assertive" and "aggressive." Here is what I found.

As-ser-tive (adjective)—confidently stating a point of view, self-assured, positively aggressive, confident, forceful, decisive, and forward.

Ag-gres-sive (adjective)—characterized by or tending toward unprovoked offensives, attacks, invasions, or the like; militantly forward or menacing or boldly assertive and forward and pushy.

The difference lies in your intent. The next time you are in a situation and you sense you might be getting a little too aggressive with people, stop and ask yourself, "What is the intention of my words, actions, and behaviors? Am I acting for the good of the whole and not my own agenda? Are my actions, words, and behavior helping or hurting others?"

I saw a poster on the Internet that seems to sum up the difference between being assertive and aggressive.

> *The difference between being assertive and aggressive is how your words and actions affect the rights of others!*
> —SHARON ANTHONY BOWER

I want to tell you about my daughter, Elke, who has always managed to stand out even as a young girl growing up. Elke is not my birth daughter, but I raised her from the time she was twelve years old. Elke came to live with Ross and me about a year after we got married when she had a major disagreement with her mother. Like with many teenage girls, there was a huge amount of tension between Elke and her mom.

Back in the early 1980s, it was rare for a father to get custody of a teenage girl, let alone a father who was recently married and his new wife was pregnant with their kid. We went through a local group, which helped fathers obtain custody of their children. All three of us went to see a psychologist to determine if we were fit to be parents and what was best for Elke. In the end, in court, the judge awarded Ross and me full custody.

Elke is a burst of life and energy. She would light up the room when she walked in full of confidence. At every report card and every teacher's conference, we would hear the same thing: "Elke lights up the room with her confidence, smile, and positive attitude."

When Elke was a teenager and starting to date, we seldom worried about her being taken advantage of by a boy. Elke was very clear about who she was and was very strong. We had a group of friends who hung out together a lot. One of the men was named Tigger, like Tigger from Winnie the Pooh (his real name was Al, but we all called him Tigger). When Elke was a teenager, she could beat Tigger arm wrestling left- and right-handed.

Elke grew up to become an incredible mom despite some ups and downs in her life. She came back to live with us when she was in her late twenties and she was in a bad situation. Elke and her two kids, David

Ross, who was about age five, and Taylor, who was age two, moved in with us in our house in Kirkland.

Elke had three things she wanted to do when she moved in: find a job, even if it was a part-time job; go back to school; and find a career she loved so she could support herself and her kids. Elke did all three with the same self-confidence and stand-out personality.

Elke continues to stand out today, and she runs the dental office where she works. Even the dentist jumps when it comes to running the office.

CHAPTER 19

PRACTICE SELF-CARE AND SELF-LOVE

Spread love wherever you go. Let no one come to
you without feeling happier when they leave!
—MOTHER TERESA

As I mentioned earlier in the book, when I was going through the fall, the counselor I was seeing recommended I read a couple of books. One was Louise Hay's *You Can Change Your Life.* I truly believe this book and several others I read really saved my life or at least saved me from a miserable and unhappy life.

I am sure my family and friends will be very surprised when they read this book and realize how bad I felt and how bad my emotional, physical, and mental health had become. As I mentioned, I was always the biggest optimist on the planet. I was always happy, smiling, and helping others. I would give and give and give until I had nothing left to give.

One of my coworkers once said about me, "There are optimists who see the glass half full. There are pessimists who see the glass half empty. You see a glass of water with a drop in it and you see the potential."

There was always one question on the different questionnaires the various doctors had me take during my quest to find out what was wrong with me. The question was "Have you ever or are you currently considering suicide?" My response to this question was not just "no" but "hell no."

The problem is my life and outside part of me everyone saw was a lie. I was actually living a lie every day. I would literally drag myself out of bed every day and try to put on my happy face, but I was miserable inside. I hated everything about myself. I still loved my family, friends, and people around me, but I truly hated myself.

I hated my body. I hated my hair. I hated my job. It took all my strength every day to get out of bed and not lie in bed all day and watch stupid TV. I was a wreck. As I mentioned, I ate poorly and gained thirty-five or more pounds. I exercised to try to stay fit, but it was a half-assed effort.

My counselor and doctor who put me on a four-month manda-tory medical leave for extreme fatigue and stress and my husband were lifesavers.

The second book I read to help me recover was Cheryl Richardson's *Extreme Self-Care*, which again I recommend for all my male and female friends and you. The book is packed full of helpful exercises and ideas on how to take care of yourself.

The book contains a lot of valuable exercises and information to help women realize that we have to take care of ourselves first, before we can really take care of others. It is simply a fact that *you can't give away what you do not own.* This is not being selfish or being a bad mother, wife, or leader; it is a fact.

My passion for helping women understand how strong they are and my quest for helping women build their self-esteem started when I worked at the bank in the late eighties and early nineties.

I started to host motivational conferences and training sessions for the non-officer staff at the bank.

I'll never forget something Bobbi Gee, the writer and motivational speaker I hired for the first women's conference said. She was a great speaker, and just like Louise Hays and Cheryl Richardson, talked about the importance of self-love and self-care.

One thing Bobbi said has stuck with me for twenty-five years. She was the one who said, "You cannot give away what you do not own." Wow... what a statement. You can't give love to your family if you don't love your-self first. You can't give forgiveness unless you forgive yourself. You can't give your kids and the people in your life love or good self-esteem unless you have good self-esteem first.

Many years ago, I read a study by the University of California Los Angeles (UCLA) on the number of negative and positive things the average child hears growing up. The study said that the average child growing up hears twenty-eight negative comments to one positive comment. Their study went on to say the average adult hears more than double the number of negative comments over positive ones as time goes on.

Things like "You call that a clean room?" and "Is that the best you can do?" go into the negative comments to our children column. Kids at school saying things like "You're stupid, fat, ugly, and so on" on the playground go into the negative column. All these kinds of comments and many more direct and more hurtful ones go into the negative column.

There are two important lessons from this research study. One, if you think you're at risk of giving your child, sister, niece, son, or any child too many compliments, you are wrong. Give the children in your life your love. Tell them they are smart, kind, and loved. Hug them often and show them you care.

The second lesson is if you are a manager, a leader, a team leader, or a leader of a project at your kids' school, tell the people you are working with the things they do well. Give them specific positive feedback and don't just say, "Good job." Tell them what they did and why it was important. Tell them you appreciate what they do, and simply say, "Thank you."

I don't mean to lie to people and tell them they did something right when they don't deserve it. I would rather be the kind of person people want to be around because they feel better after we work together on something than someone who is a Debbie Downer and makes people feel worse.

I am sure most people have seen the show called *American Idol* or some international version of this show like *Britain's Idol* or even *Singapore Idol*, which we watched when I worked in the Asia Pacific region. Each one of these shows has a consistent format. There are three or four judges, and one is usually very harsh in his or her feedback to the contestants. And there are usually some really bad singers.

One season on *American Idol*, there was a woman singer who was simply terrible. Her voice was like fingernails on a chalkboard. Simon Cowell, the very critical judge, asked this woman if she had a singing coach. The woman responded that she did.

Simon looked at her and said, "You should fire her because you are a terrible singer and you should get a lawyer and sue her." If you've seen the new *America's Got Talent* show with Simon, you would see now how mellow he has become as a dad.

The point is everyone has some redeeming qualities, and your job is to find them.

CHAPTER 20

THE POWER OF POSITIVE AFFIRMATIONS

*A woman is the full circle. Within her is the
power to create, nurture, and transform!*
—DIANE MARIECHILD

One of my favorite employees when I worked at the bank was a young woman named Misty. When I interviewed Misty, she walked into my office and pulled the desk chair across the room and put it right in front of my desk. She said, "I'm ready, and you should hire me."

I hired her on the spot, and she was one of my best hires. When I would be out of the office for a few days in our headquarters in Los Angeles, I would leave notes on her desk, telling her how wonderful she was and how much I appreciated everything she did to help in the department. When I was in the office, I would tell her what a great job she was doing and thank her every time she did something for me.

It was performance appraisal time and time for me to sit down with Misty and give her feedback about how she'd been performing the last year. It was a very good performance appraisal, but partway through the meeting, she started to cry.

I was shocked and stopped to ask her what was wrong because I had given her a very good review and was going to promote her and give her a raise.

Her response was, "No one ever told me these kinds of things before. I grew up with an alcoholic mother and an abusive father. All I heard every day was how stupid, ugly, fat, and worthless I was. You are the first person to ever tell me I am worthy, smart, and a good person."

I walked around my desk, hugged her, and said, "You are important to me and the best employee I've ever worked with. Thank you." Misty went on to flourish at the bank and turned out to be a wonderful and successful person. I often wonder what happened to her after I left the bank.

The message here is simple: find something good in everyone you work with, interact with, or meet. Tell people the good things they do and simply say, "Thank you" a little more often. Be the kind of person you want to hang out with every day.

So how do you build up your self-confidence and self-esteem? One way is to surround yourself with positive people who love you and find ways to build you up and not tear you down. Second, practice and use positive affirmations combined with action to build yourself into the person or leader you want to be.

There are hundreds of books written on the power of positive affirmations, and I do believe they work *if* you put action behind the affirmations.

Positive affirmations are the good things we say to ourselves either out loud or silently. I often ask people in one of my sessions if they talk to themselves. I usually get mixed responses of head nods and head shakes. I then ask, "For those of you who said no, my questions is, who did you talk to when I asked whether or not you talk to yourself."

The simple fact is we all have an inner voice that tells us we are doing well or we need improvement. The problem is just like the UCLA study on the number of negatives to positives that a child hears, we probably hear more negative thoughts than positive ones; this is especially true for women.

A positive affirmation is always stated in present tense as if it is already true. One thing Louise Hay recommends in her book, *You Can Change Your Life*, is doing what she calls "mirror work," which is standing in front of a mirror and saying, "I love you, (insert your name)," and repeating a few positive affirmations several times a day.

Affirmations and How to Use Them

The power of the spoken word can't be underestimated when you are looking to deliberately attract positive change in your life and be the best leader you can be.

Words are largely responsible for the people we are today. The words we use to describe ourselves as well as the words others use to describe us have a significant impact on the people we grow up to be.

Be it a positive or a negative word or sentence, it can plant a seed within the brain that when watered enough with enough attention over time will grow into reality.

It is important to note that the subconscious mind cannot tell the difference between a fact and something that is imagined. Therefore, if you spend your lifetime saying, "I am no good at math," or "I am not a creative person," to describe yourself, whether it is true or not, this is what will manifest in your life.

In order to emit a different frequency, you need to begin to choose your words differently. If you don't like the song playing on the radio, you need to change the channel. This is where positive affirmations come in.

What Are Affirmations?

An affirmation is a word or statement repeated over time in the present tense as if it were true. When we use positive affirmations, we are trying to tune our internal radio to the right channel so we can dance or sing. This is why it is important that when we say our positive affirmations, we say them as if we've already achieved our goals.

For example, I've struggled with my weight since I was about eight years old. Prior to age eight, my parents kept taking me to different doctors, trying to figure out why I was so small and could not gain weight. I finally started to gain weight, but I spent my teen and my adult life always losing and gaining weight.

My positive affirmations are focused on being fit and making good food choices. My new affirmations are the following:

"I love having a fit and healthy body."
"I make healthy food choices and love to work out."

Repetition is the key. You need to say your positive affirmations to yourself several times a day. This is because the more we say something, the more we believe it. The more we tell ourselves we are smart and talented, the more ingrained the new thought becomes in our minds.

Three Steps to Using Positive Affirmations

1. Write down your positive affirmations. Write affirmations that are goal oriented and in the present tense as if you have already achieved them.
2. Believe in it. In order to attract positive change into your life, you need to be emitting positive signals. Feel good while you say your affirmations to yourself. Really listen to the words and allow the positivity in what you are saying to wash over you.
3. Repeat often. The more you say the positive affirmations, the truer they become for you. Repetition creates new beliefs, and the more you say them, the more real they will become for you.

Tips for Using Positive Affirmations

Put your positive affirmations all over your house and work area. I have small nice journals all over my house. It put them in my makeup drawer so I see them in the morning and at night when I wash my face before bed. Put them on your refrigerator. I have some positive affirmations inside my cover for my e-book reader so I see them every time I pick up my e-reader.

Use positive affirmations that are believable and important to you. Try saying thank you to yourself after you say each affirmation. Practice your positive affirmations first thing in the morning and last thing at night.

Concentrate on a few positive affirmations at a time. I usually have three to five that I repeat for a month, and then I add or change a few and keep going. Focusing on a few key affirmations at one time will prevent you from getting overwhelmed.

Here are a few of my specific positive affirmations as an example. Later in the section, I'll have you write your own.

- I am strong and talented and can do anything I put my mind to do.
- I believe in myself and my unique talents.
- I cross each new bridge with ease.
- I love myself more every day.
- My dreams are worthy.
- I love working out and being fit.
- I make healthy food choices to perform at my best.
- My vision is strong and guides me to do the right thing.
- I ask the best of myself and the world, and I get it.
- I am empowered with strength, wisdom, and spirit to do anything I set out to do.

The Little Things Women Sometimes Do

Stop being afraid of what could go wrong and start being positive about what could go right!
—ANONYMOUS

One of the things I hear and see often is women putting themselves down, and sometimes they are not aware they are doing it. One of the ways I've seen a number of women put themselves down is by saying things like "I am *just* an administrative assistant," or "I am *only* a stay-at-home mom," or "I am *just* a team leader," or "I am only a [fill in the blank]."

We need to work together to stop using "only" and "just" to describe ourselves or other women. Simply avoid the extra word and say, "I am an executive assistant," or "I am a team leader." Period. Don't add extra words that put yourself or others down.

Another thing that has been pointed out to me by a number of people is women tend to say, "I'm sorry," too often, even when things are not our fault. I know I fall into this category from time to time. If we get lost, I'll say I'm sorry when it is not my fault my husband took a wrong turn.

It is OK to say you're sorry when something is your fault, or, better yet, replace "I'm sorry" with "I apologize." If you accidently bump into someone, rather than say, "I'm sorry," say "Excuse me." Just a few thoughts to consider.

One more thing, learn to say, "Thank you," when someone compliments you. Many times when someone compliments me on a dress or tells me I look good today, I respond, "Oh, this old dress? I bought it at Target three years ago."

When someone gives you a compliment, they are giving you a gift. Don't take that gift away by rationalizing anything. Again, just say, "Thank you."

Be Grateful and Keep a Gratitude Journal

Oprah Winfrey, Louise Hay, motivational speakers, and highly successful business leaders all talk about being grateful for the many blessings in their lives. Some people might need to search deep into their past to find these blessings to be grateful for, but they are there. Other people could fill ten college notebook pages with list upon list of things to be grateful for in life.

Every leader I interviewed talked about someone or something she was grateful for in her life. It might have been a manager, a parent, or a mentor, but someone helped her become the leader and person she is today.

Remember the exercise you completed earlier on the person or people who influenced you when you were going up? I remember one leader I worked for at the bank who was a great leader. Larry was firm but fair and always pushed me to do better because he knew what I was capable of doing.

I have to admit there were times when we were arguing over the best way to complete a project or accomplish a task, and I did not like Larry or think he was a great leader. People would walk by his office as we were almost yelling at each other and say, "If the two of you are going to argue so loudly, can you please close the door?"

One of the two of us would look at the person a bit confused and say, "We're not arguing; we're trying to fix a hard problem." We'd both laugh and keep arguing.

Several years later, I invited Larry to lunch to thank him for being a tough son of a bitch and helping me become a better leader.

Keep a Gratitude Folder for Yourself and Your Team

One of the things my good friend Cynthia reminded me of was the power of a "gratitude file," either a computer document or an old-fashioned paper one. The purpose of a gratitude file is to remind ourselves of all the good things we've accomplished over the years.

I forgot that I suggested a gratitude file to Cynthia a long time ago when we worked at the bank as a way to stay personally motivated and upbeat. Every time you get a nice e-mail, letter, or compliment, put a copy in your gratitude file.

There are two reasons for doing this:

1. When you are feeling down about how things are going in your life, you review your folder and remind yourself about all the good things you've accomplished.
2. If you work and it is time for the wonderful annual performance review, you have good examples of the things you accomplished that year when it comes time to write your review.

Here is an example of an e-mail from one of Cynthia's clients, which she keeps in her gratitude folder.

Hi, Cynthia,

Thank you for extending your valuable time to meet with me. I went to the Central Library to borrow Pink and Lencioni's books. I hope to discuss our opinions on these topics the next time we meet.

I was telling my parents about you and how much resemblance there is between you and my father—honorable, wise, and kind-hearted. I am especially thankful for your values in education. For learners like myself, it is rare that we cross paths with a teacher like you who is willing to invest and develop us.

I hope you see potential in me to strengthen me personally and professionally as I walk through this journey of converging my passions.

Please let me know if anything else comes to your mind for good reads or research that you find essential for me to do.

Sincerely, S

When I was a manager, I used to keep a gratitude folder on all my employees. If you are a manager and need to provide feedback or write performance reviews, this information is invaluable and gives you a lot of evidence and reminders of all the things your employee did during the year. It makes the review process easier.

Gratitude Exercise—I Am Grateful for the Following in My Life

Most inspirational books and leaders talk about keeping a gratitude journal, and I started this formally when I was recovering from my fall. I would write down five things I was grateful for each morning and evening. I would read these items out loud every morning and evening. When we moved recently, I found my gratitude journals all over the house.

Now, your challenge is to buy a nice journal or notebook. For the next thirty days, write down five things you are grateful for every morning and every evening. Read them aloud in front of a mirror or in your favorite peaceful place.

My Morning Gratitude Statements

1. _____
2. _____
3. _____
4. _____
5. _____

My Evening Gratitude Statements

1. _____
2. _____
3. _____
4. _____
5. _____

CHAPTER 21

FORGIVE AND FORGET AND LET IT GO

Have you been punishing yourself or someone for something that happened years ago? Are you holding a grudge that does not pay off in the long run and causes you personal and professional harm? There is no value in carrying a grudge around, only a weighty price.

Many years ago, a friend and colleague of mine Cynthia and I did a lot of research into the difference between stress and peak performance.

We found that one person in a certain situation would be in peak performance mode and excelling. A different person in the same situation would be totally stressed.

We did some research into what happens when we are stressed out versus what happens when we are in our peak performance zone. We found a number of interesting biological facts. When the body is in a state of stress, anger, and rage, all kinds of chemicals are released into the body. The body has a natural fight-or-flight response, which dates back to the caveman and cavewoman days.

In one situation, one person wants to flee or leave the uncomfortable and stressful situation and another person wants to stay and fight. A third person might react to the situation by choosing not to fight or flee but to "go with the flow."

Remember I said I have a strange, almost freakish habit of wanting to know where things come from earlier in the book? I went on another quest to understand what the word *react* means.

Here is what the word *react* means: "to act without thinking." So every time you react to something, you are thinking without your head. Better yet, you've engaged your mouth without your brain, and how often does that turn out good for you or anyone involved?

Forgiveness means being strong and letting go of something that happened in the past, sometimes things that happened years ago. Our pain in most cases does not come from what happened to us but from holding on to the pain and the painful memories. The fact is you can't change what happened to you in the past, but you can change how you react, respond, and choose to live. Better yet, you can learn from it like every woman I interviewed told me.

It is within our power to change. It is within our power to release the negative thoughts and to forgive ourselves and others. You can release the negative thoughts that are holding you back. You can choose to let go of negative thoughts that are holding back. You can say, "I choose to change thoughts that hurt me."

Research shows it takes between twenty-eight and thirty days to change a habit or pattern of thinking. To be honest, I think it takes a lot longer, or at least it took me several months of continuous practice to change some of my negative thinking.

We all hold on to things, events, or people in life we need to forgive and forget. Just like the song from *Frozen*, we need to "Let It Go." I heard that song so many times when the movie came out. I would change the channel so I didn't hear the song for the one-hundredth time that day. It is actually a very good song with great lyrics about letting go of things that are holding us back. I just could not stand the idea of hearing it one more time.

Another exercise I completed when I was recovering from my fall was to forgive someone for something he or she did to me a long time ago. I needed to find someone in my life I needed to talk to and tell him or her how I felt in the past when he or she did something that still bothered me today.

I recall I was very angry at my mom one time because she would not buy me a special new dress for the school's big homecoming dance. She told me I had a lot of formal dresses from other dances and from the dresses I wore being a Rainbow Girl so I did not need a new dress.

I was upset at the time and held on to that anger for many years. I felt she was telling me I was not important enough or did not deserve a new dress for one night. I recall my dad would always tell me when my mom would get really tight with money to remember she grew up as a child during the Depression with a dad who was a coal miner in West Virginia and Ohio and they were very poor. Yes, my mom was a coal miner's daughter, just like the Loretta Lynn country song.

Because of how she was raised, Mom had a couple of funny habits or quirks. One of her habits was when something went on sale for a good price, like coffee, toilet paper, or Campbell's Soup, she would buy cases of it. She would stock all this stuff on shelves in our garage. She had a fear that we would run out of something or have to pay a higher price. She grew up in a large family, and they had to struggle for everything, so money was precious to her.

She was also the only girl. She struggled as a child, and I know she always meant well and tried to do what was best for me. Through her many lessons, she was teaching me to face my fears and issues head-on and with gusto. To my mom, a new dress for a special occasion was a luxury and not needed when I had several almost new long formal dresses I could wear.

In order to forgive my mom and learn to let go, I sat down with my journal on the floor in our spare bedroom. I wrote what had happened, how I felt, and why what she did still bothered me. Part of the exercise was to talk to this person directly or if he or she had passed, talk to a mirror.

So as silly as it sounds, I sat on the floor in my spare bedroom and talked to my mom since she had passed away years before. I cried, I laughed, and I let it go.

I decided to let go, find a fresh perspective, and be my own boss. I decided that my mom was doing the best she could to raise me to be a strong and independent woman. She was encouraging me to be strong, and I decided to take this lesson and all her lessons to me as lessons of love.

There is a process to letting go and forgiving yourself or others.

1. Acknowledge the hurt. Give yourself permission to be angry for a certain period of time. Cry, yell, talk to a trusted friend, hit a pillow, or do what you need to do to get over the anger. You need

to let it out to genuinely get over the hurt and anger. Holding it in is not healthy and can lead to some physically and emotionally damaging results. Just don't stay in this stage for too long.

2. Let go of "if-thens." My husband has a saying he used to repeat to the boys on the football team when they would say, "If such-and-such happened, then I would have made that touchdown." My husband's saying was, "If then or buts were candy and nuts, we'd all have a Merry Christmas." The boys would look at him as if he were crazy, laugh, and walk away. One research study said 60 percent of Americans said they would only forgive someone if he or she apologized. To be honest, that might not ever happen in some cases and with some people. You may need to be the brave one who takes the first steps and forgives someone so you don't carry that pain around anymore.

3. Rewrite your story. It is OK to share your grievances with a trusted friend, coworker, or family member; just don't throw a pity party. Don't try to convince others to join your side. Don't try to get them to dislike the person as much as you do or try to recruit others to your cause. Doing so is a self-defeating behavior and will not make the situation better or go away.

4. Try a little empathy. This might be hard for many people, but I worked for the worst manager on earth. Once my friend Meredith told me that the problem was with him and not me, I actually started to feel sorry for him and his family. Finding a way to humanize or express a little empathy for the other person can make it easier to let go of the bitterness and help you move on.

5. Don't try to zip through the process. Depending on the situation, it can take days, weeks, months, and even years to forgive someone and just let it go. You have to go at your own pace. I did not forgive my mom for the homecoming dress incident until I was an adult, married, and she had passed away.

The mind and body benefit, will allow you to be a better leader when you begin to get rid of the bitterness and self-pity, one hurtful feeling at a time. However, there is a heavy fine to pay for holding on to grudges and hurt feeling too long, both emotionally and physically.

For example, you are headed to your high school reunion and you know one of the girls you did not get along with will be there. In high school, she was always talking down to you and making fun of you in front of your friends. Here is what happens to you when you meet her years later at the reunion.

1. The part of your brain that processes emotions sends out a message: "Danger!" Then your adrenal glands get a green light to flood your body with stress hormones.
2. Your cortisol level rises and you get into a fight-or-flight mode, increasing your blood sugar levels and suppressing your immune system.
3. Your blood pressure and heart rate speed up, which results in your blood vessels narrowing. This makes blood clot more easily and can lead to a heart attack or stroke.
4. Finally, you start to calm down, but the damage is done. Constant high cortisol levels prompt your body to store belly fat, which makes it harder to lose weight and can lead to diabetes.

Maybe it's time to practice a little forgiveness with ourselves and others in order to be strong, effective, and healthy female leaders. Here is a great thought to remember:

"Don't let negative and toxic people rent space in your head. Raise the rent and kick them out!"

I saw the following great quote in my recent issue of *Oprah* magazine. The quote was from Elizabeth Gilbert, from her book, *Big Magic.*

I have a welcoming speech prepared for fear,
which I deliver right before embarking upon a new project...
Dearest Fear: Creativity and I are about
to go on a road trip together.
I understand you'll be joining us, because you always do...
You're allowed to take a seat, and you're allowed to have a voice,
but you're not allowed a vote!

Try saying this to yourself or out loud in your mirror or in your car for the next thirty days or longer.

> "I declare today and every day going forward as my declaration day. Give me the willingness to let go of the past and begin to think anew. I will face my fears with gusto and look at things from a fresh perspective!"

CHAPTER 22

BEING THE BEST LEADER YOU CAN BE

Don't believe you have to be a better leader than other people.
Just believe you have to be a better leader
than you were yesterday!
—ANONYMOUS

I mentioned you can learn a lot about being a great leader by watching and learning from the leaders around you. A great leader in your life might have been a teacher, a coach, a music teacher, a manager, or even your parents. They can all be great role models to follow.

I worked for a great female leader at work named Deb. Deb was an amazingly compassionate woman who was smart and a great teacher, motivator, and coach. She would praise you and make sure you got the right recognition when warranted.

Deb would also tell me when I was heading down the wrong path and about to make a mistake. If I had a problem with another department or group, she would give me the right advice and step in to help when I needed it.

I remember the great leadership qualities Deb possessed. I remember how empowered and motivated I felt to do a good job for her and myself. I loved Deb as a leader so much that when I was considering moving to a different group and found out the manager I was going to be reporting to in the new department was leaving, I contacted Deb and convinced her she should apply for this manager job so I could continue to report to her.

Deb became a coach and mentor even after I no longer worked for her. When I told her I wanted to take an international assignment at Microsoft, she helped me find a great job in Asia. I frequently tell people and Deb publicly that she was my favorite manager.

On the other hand, I've had two really bad managers in my long career. The worst manager I ever worked for was a man I'll call "Dick" at the bank. I frequently talk about Dick in my leadership training programs and describe him as a paranoid schizophrenic with masochistic tendencies.

Dick was the kind of person who would criticize people in public and literally yell at people in front of others. When I made vice president at the bank, he walked by my department yelling, "Grimm, you've really done it this time." He grabbed me by the lapel of my jacket and threw me into my office. Once he closed the door, he said, "Congratulations! You just made VP!" and walked out.

There were five vice presidents who all reported to him. We figured out Dick had a pattern to his rants and raves. He would pick one of us and literally beat on the person all day. We figured out Monday was one person's day of beating, Tuesday was someone else's, and so on.

We all protected each other on the chosen day and would make excuses for why that person was out of the office. We all got together and formed a Breakfast Club. We would meet for breakfast once a week to figure out how to manage around him and survive. We helped each other, coached each other, encouraged each other, and assured each other that the problem was not us but him.

I lived in South Orange County and worked in San Diego. I had a sixty-four-mile drive each way down the coast of California. There were days I would cry most of the way home. On my drive to work, I could feel my stress level going up as I got closer to the office, wondering if today was my day.

I almost quit a couple of times but decided I was strong enough and wanted to stay to finish some important work I had started. Two things happened to change my view and helped me not just survive but thrive.

First, a good friend, Meredith, would listen to my complaints when I would tell her the latest beating I had endured that week. She was a very insightful person. One day, as she listened to my latest beating, she said, "I know what the problem is. The problem is not you; the problem is Dick."

She continued, "You see, people like Dick have a big ego combined with a low self-esteem. The only way they feel good is to make you and others feel bad."

I felt like I'd been hit by a skillet. This simple statement completely changed my attitude and how I responded to Dick.

I had allowed him to impact my self-esteem and self-confidence. I started to question myself and my capabilities. If Dick would start to yell at me, I would back down and not fight back. People who know me may find this hard to believe, but I became a cautious introvert.

After my conversation with Meredith, I started to fight back when I knew I was right. One day, I was out of my office at a meeting in Los Angeles for a few days. When I got back to my office, my entire staff was standing outside the building waiting for me.

I found out that while I was in Los Angeles, Dick had decided to take his anger out on my staff. They told me he yelled at them all day and how badly they felt.

I was so livid I walked up three flights of stairs to Dick's office because the elevator would take too long. I walked into his office and said, "If you ever do that to my staff again, I'll kill you." Today, I probably would have been arrested for workplace violence, but back in the late eighties workplace violence was not so common.

A few years later, after I left the bank as a full-time employee, I was teaching the bank's off-site leadership course. Dick was a participant in one of the programs I was teaching. In one of the team exercises, he cheated. He cheated on a simple team-building exercise, and the rest of the participants called him out on his poor behavior.

I also heard years later, Dick was fired from the bank for doing the same kind of thing to a woman who was an executive with one of the bank's biggest suppliers.

When I teach my leadership workshops, I always tell my story about Dick as an example of a bad manager. I usually have people do two things to understand how a leader's actions impact the performances and results of their people.

First, I ask people to think about the best leader or manager they've ever worked for in their life and answer the following questions:

1. What did the leader do?
2. How did you feel?
3. How did this impact on your performance?

Second, I ask people to think about the worst leader or manager they've ever worked for in their life and answer the following questions:

1. What did the leader do?
2. How did you feel?
3. How did this impact on your performance?

One interesting observation someone pointed out recently was they had to think really hard and back a long time into their career to come up with the best leader or manager. However, the name, face, and experience with the bad leader or manager came to mind immediately.

Here is how badly and strongly my memory of Dick still impacts me today. My office was right next to the training rooms since I was in charge of the employee and manager training programs. Outside the training room and next to my office was the coffee machine. This was the kind of coffee machine you see in a restaurant with the pots on burners.

When the coffee would get really low, the coffee would get a strong burned smell. If I was away from my desk or the door was closed, I sometimes did not notice the coffee was burning.

Dick would come by my desk and scream at me to fix the effing coffee machine again. He said he was sick of the smell and it might cause a fire. He was probably right about the fire thing.

To this day, I smell that burning coffee on the burner and I remember Dick.

Here is the key leadership lesson from this exercise. Watch, observe, and learn from the great leaders and managers. Adopt or adapt what these managers did to your style. Don't try to copy them but learn from what they did. Sometimes when we try to copy someone's style, it comes across as not genuine or phony and does not last.

However, I tell people to remember what the bad leader or manager did, how they felt, and how it impacted on their performance. The performance of people under this kind of leader or manager may improve for a short time out of fear, but long term, people simply become disengaged, quit, or quit on the job.

My final suggestion to people on their bad leader or manager experience is to remember how they felt and how it impacted their performance and ask themselves why they would pass this along to anyone else.

Positive and kind words can empower, encourage,
motivate, and help move someone toward their goals.
Always choose words that can heal not destroy!
—ANURANG PRAKASH

CHAPTER 23

THE POWER OF FEEDBACK

A key part of any leader's job is to provide feedback to his or her followers. It is an important part of the job, and according to recent research by Gallup, frequent feedback is even more important to millennials.

Keeping in mind my earlier research on what makes an effective female leader, characteristics like being a great developer of people, valuing diverse styles and people, and being compassionate are areas where we as women in leadership can soar.

There is a wonderful leadership video and book by James Autry called *Love and Profit—The Art of Caring Leadership*. I love this book and video and show the video in my leadership workshops. James Autry is not a management consultant, guru, or college professor. He was a businessman who ran one of the most successful publishing companies in the United States.

In his video and book, James outlines the five leadership essentials. Here is my interpretation of his five leadership essentials.

1. Avoid "in-box" management.
2. Special treatment
3. Be honest.
4. Trust your employees.
5. If you don't like management, get out before it is too late.

Let's take a look at each one of these and see how they apply to being a great female leader.

1. Avoid "in-box" management. Stop sitting at your desk and managing your business and people by monitoring your in-box and waiting for something to go wrong so you have something important to do. Get out of your office and walk around. Talk to people, coach them, and support them in the moment.

   If you are regularly available and present with your people, you'll have fewer surprises and fires to put out. The size and number of mistakes will shrink.

2. Practice special treatment. We talked about special treatment earlier when we talked about personal styles. Great leaders coach people the way they want to be coached. They coach people in the moment, not six months or a year later at performance appraisal time.

   Sorry for the sports analogy, but it works in this case. Great coaches coach people before, during, and after the game. They don't wait until the game is over and coach to the scoreboard. There is nothing the leader or the team member can do to change the score once the game is over. Great coaches are on the field and coaching the team throughout the game.

   Great coaches realize not everyone is hardwired the same way and there are certain jobs that are better for one individual or person than another. Not everyone has the same strengths, as we discussed earlier in the book. Great leaders play to their team's strengths and put people in jobs where they can excel.

3. Be honest. According to James Autry, honesty is the most important attribute between a leader and his or her followers. This is really important when you need to tell someone their performance is not up to speed or they are falling behind in their work. If you really care about the person, you need to be honest with him or her and yourself.

   You need to follow the coaching with CARE model, and you have to be able to say honestly, "Judy, I care about you and about your work. I need to tell you that you are not performing according to our agreed-upon standards."

   Not being upfront with employees and not telling them when they are not performing well is being dishonest with them, the team, and yourself. Sometimes you have to put someone on disciplinary action or even fire him or her. It is a very tough thing to do but it is part of being a leader.

4. Trust your employees. I am willing to bet there is no one who comes to work every day saying, "I think I'll screw up today." There might be a few people who feel that way, depending on how they are being treated, but 99.9 percent of the people come to work wanting to do a good job.

    You need to trust your people to do the work they were hired to do. Your job is to coach them to reach their full potential, not do their job.

5. Finally, my favorite, if you don't love people, get out of it before it is too late. There are some people who move into management roles solely for the money or title. That is the wrong reason to want to become a manager or leader.

    James Autry says, "I mean it. Save yourself the heart attack and save many other people from the daily grief. I always tell my supervisors—people want to know how much you care, before they care how much you know." Wise words from a wise leader.

Good communication skills are required to be a great leader—male or female leader, period. Communicating openly and honestly is always listed in the top ten in every leadership survey. It is an essential leadership skill that separates the average manager or leader from an extraordinary leader.

I don't know about you, but I would rather be viewed as an extraordinary leader than an average one. You can't inspire and motivate people to follow you or your vision if you can't clearly articulate your vision in a way they can understand.

For some of us, giving positive feedback to someone for a job well done is easy and enjoyable. But what about telling someone he or she is not performing well or is doing a poor job?

You are doing the nonperforming employee a disservice by not letting him or her know where he or she can improve and helping him or her get better. In addition, you are hurting the rest of your team, yourself, the organization you work for, and your customers.

I've personally seen it, when the leader finally has the courage to let the poor performer go and the rest of the team either says, "Thank you," or says, "It is about time you noticed [insert name] was destroying the entire team."

Being a leader means being willing to do the right thing even when the right thing is hard. The leader's role is to set standards of excellence and coach his or her people to reach these standards. There are times the right thing to do is let someone go or fire him or her.

I had a teller named Glenna who could not balance her cash drawer or do the other required parts of the job. I took Glenna aside four or five times to coach her on how to do the job. I finally needed to fire Glenna for the good of the team and myself as the leader.

Six months after I fired Glenna, she walked into the branch. At first, I was concerned she might be upset and might have come back to yell at me for firing her. Instead, she wanted to thank me since it turned out Glenna was an alcoholic and the alcohol was affecting her eyesight. Glenna thanked me for firing her, and she told me that because I fired her, she went to AA and had been sober for six months.

> *Positive and kind words can empower, encourage,*
> *motivate, and help move someone toward their goals.*
> *Always choose words that can heal not destroy!*
> —ANITA RODDICK, FOUNDER, THE BODY SHOP

Personal Leadership Action Plan Part 5
Complete the exercise described in this section.

1. Think about the best leader or manager you've ever worked for in your life and answer the following questions:
   - What did the leader do?

   - How did you feel?

   - How did this impact on your performance?

2. Think about the worst leader or manager you've ever worked for in your life and answer the following questions:
    - What did the leader do?

    - How did you feel?

    - How did this impact on your performance?

As I stated earlier, you learn how to be a great leader by following the actions of the great leaders who inspired you. You also learn from the bad leaders in your life. You learn never to be that kind of leader and never to treat the people you lead in this way.

Women Stand Out When Leading Millennials

When it comes to leading millennials, women have a natural advantage over most men, given our strengths. I imagine when many of us Baby Boomers were coming into the workplace, the managers and leaders before us had a hard time understanding our needs and leading us because we grew up in a very different environment.

The same is true for millennials. When they grew up, they always had a color TV with hundreds of channels and a remote control. They've always had computers and cell phones in their lives. Our future and the future of our children and grandchildren will someday lie in the hands of the millennials, who will be the leaders of our companies and countries soon. We need to learn how to work with them and lead them.

The average baby boomer surfs the Internet on his or her computer. The average millennial surfs the Internet from his or her phone. Millennials are less likely to watch conventional TV, so advertising companies might be missing the mark spending billions of dollars on expensive traditional TV ads.

Here are some interesting facts about millennials from a recent Gallup white paper *How Millennials Want to Live and Work*.

1. Millennials were born between 1980 and 1996.
2. They want good jobs, but they struggle to find good jobs that engage them.

3. They are highly educated, and they have the highest rate of unemployment and underemployment.
4. Millennials want coaches, not bosses or managers.
5. Millennials want to have a purpose to their work beyond a paycheck.
6. Only 29 percent of millennials are engaged at work.
7. Millennials are the most wired generation.
8. Millennials need to be able to have access to the latest technology and tools.
9. Millennial turnover due to lack of engagement costs the US economy $30.5 billion annually.

Here is the disturbing fact, while it is every parent's dream to have his or her child lead a better life than he or she did, not all millennials are positioned correctly to do so. Our children or millennials might be the first generation that is not better off than their parents.

Let's face it; the annual performance appraisal is an outdated concept. I used to joke in my coaching workshops that the three words managers and employees hated equally were "annual performance appraisal"—similar to the three words parents hate the most on Christmas morning, "batteries not included."

The annual performance process is even more ineffective with millennials. Face it; they grew up in a wired world where feedback is frequent, delivered instantly, and received in a second, not once a year. They require constant feedback. Millennials are more engaged when the coaching they receive is frequent and consistent.

A few other facts worth noting about millennials. They want more than a paycheck; they want a purpose to their work. On average, millennials are not pursuing job satisfaction; they are pursuing development. Research shows a millennial will leave one job for another not just for pay but for pay and the opportunity for development.

Remember, millennials don't want bosses; they want a coach to care about them and develop their skills. Here is a staggering fact on millennials: 87 percent of millennials said development is the most important thing in a job, as compared to 48 percent of baby boomers.

> MILLENNIALS WHO SAY DEVELOPMENT IS
> IMPORTANT IN A JOB
>
> # 87%
>
> GALLUP

Millennials don't want to fix their weaknesses; they want to develop their strengths. A leader can't ignore weaknesses, but rather than focus on the millennials' weaknesses, they should focus on maximizing their strengths and minimizing their weaknesses. Use the knowledge you gained in the "Be Strong" section to find the right job to fit the millennials' strengths.

Finally, millennials want a good job and a place that values their unique talents and contributions. Millennials want to know, "Does this company value my strengths and give me a chance to do what I do best every day?"

Leading millennials is an area where female leaders have an advantage and can put their skills to work to help them fit into the world at large. One suggestion is to find a millennial to mentor and develop. He or she might be able to teach you a few things too, like how to use Twitter, Instagram, and Snapchat and how to fix your phone.

We'll talk about mentoring in more detail in the last section of the book.

Personal Leadership Action Plan 6

Here are a few things you can do to improve your communication skills:

1. Take a class on being a good communicator.
2. Buy some books, or check them out from the library.
3. Increase your confidence by joining Toastmasters, which is a worldwide organization to help people improve their speaking skills.
4. Practice giving short speeches at local community or charity groups.

CHAPTER 24

THE MYTH OF DOING IT ALL

Let's talk about a few myths that are out there for many women. Cinderella was a character in a Disney movie, and Superwoman was a Marvel comic character. Let's face it; we can't do it all. We can't be the perfect woman, the perfect leader, the perfect team player, the perfect wife or significant other, *and* the perfect mom. Trust me; I tried, and it almost killed me.

There was a popular book for women called *The Cinderella Complex: Women's Hidden Fear of Independence* by Colette Dowling back in 1981. The book made the point that you can't do it all. No one, man or woman, can be perfect at everything, and trying to do this leads to nothing but disappointment.

I said this earlier but let me say it again: "You can't give away what you do not own." You have to put yourself first so you have the energy to help others around you. Putting yourself first is not selfish; it is a matter of personal survival over the long haul.

I was always guilty of trying to do it all at work and would many times put aside some of my work in order to help others. I would help them out at work, and then I would go home and try to finish my work after dinner, late at night, or on the weekend.

I went to a doctor many years ago who told me I needed to eat better, sleep more, and take better care of myself. At the time, I looked at him as if he were totally mad and said, "How can I do that? I have a very demanding full-time job, and I am a mom and wife. I don't have time to eat better, sleep more, and take better care of myself."

The fact is the doctor was 100 percent right in his diagnosis. When I had my fall and my stumble a year or so later, I realized I had stopped taking care of myself first. I let other people's priorities be more important than my own health and well-being.

Something had to give, and I did not want it to be me again. I had to set boundaries and decided I needed to invest in working out, eating right, getting at least seven hours of sleep a night, living my vision, and investing in my own learning.

I had to work out a deal with my family and husband that I could not do it all myself and needed their help. I am not a very good housekeeper, and this is one skill I don't care to try to improve. I need help with the grocery shopping, cooking, and cleaning. I had to do something very hard for most women. I needed to ask for help and admit I could not do it all.

I set boundaries that I would not do e-mail first thing in the morning until I went through my morning routine. I no longer do e-mail in the evening or on weekends, unless I choose to do something for myself. I also do "time blocking" on my calendar. I set a time limit on when I check e-mail in the morning and the late afternoon and shut down my e-mail during the other times.

I blocked out personal time early in the morning to work out and read an inspiring book or something silly and fun. I started to read for fun and not for work. I set time to go for a walk with my dog or to go to the beach.

Personal and Leadership Action Plan 7

1. Write your positive affirmations and practice them at least twice a day.
2. Get your gratitude journal and write out five things you are grateful for in your life.
3. Practice being the kind of leader James Autry talks about in *Love and Profit.*
4. Take a look at your calendar and time block your schedule to put yourself first on your to-do list.

SECTION 5
SUMMARY AND FINAL ACTION PLAN

She's just a girl, and she's on fire
Hotter than a fantasy, longer like a highway
She's living in a world, and it's on fire
Feeling the catastrophe, but she knows she can fly away
Oh, she got both feet on the ground
And she's burning it down
Oh, she got her head in the clouds
And she's not backing down
This girl is on fire
This girl is on fire
She's walking on fire
This girl is on fire

Looks like a girl, but she's a flame
So bright, she can burn your eyes
Better look the other way
You can try but you'll never forget her name
She's on top of the world
Hottest of the hottest girls say
Oh, we got our feet on the ground
And we're burning it down
Oh, got our head in the clouds
And we're not coming down
—ALICIA KEYS, "GIRL ON FIRE"

CHAPTER 25

EVA'S STORY

Control your own destiny; otherwise someone else will.
Why would you give that power to anyone else?
— PATTIE GRIMM

E va was an early pioneer and glass breaker. Eva grew up in war-torn London, and her childhood was disrupted by the frequent bombings of World War II. Things did not get much better after the war because of the extreme shortages of many food staples, like meat, fruit, vegetables, and milk.

Eva's creative idea to get out of the terrible circumstances in England was to get a job as one of the first flight attendants and be able to travel the world. She lied in the interview about being able to speak a second language and was hired to join the first crew of the South America Airways, a new airline scheduled to fly between London and South America. The planes were not the 777s we see today. The planes were converted military aircrafts with no seat belts or airbags.

Eva continued to fly to some of the world's most exotic places until she fell in love and married her husband. In order to help support the family, Eva started to run several businesses out of her home. She ran one successful business until the government shut her business down. She could have given up, but she chose to find another business to open and then another one and another one.

Eva raised a wonderful family as she continued to find new and creative ways to run a business or make money. Eva had a son named Richard. She always wanted her children to be independent and creative thinkers. One day, on the way home from town, Eva decided to drop five-year-old Richard off a couple of miles from home and let him find his way home by himself.

I know this would be frowned upon in today's dangerous world, but this was a long time ago, and they lived in rural England at the time. As it started to get dark, Eva began to wonder if she had done the wrong thing and if she and her husband should go looking for Richard. After about fifteen minutes, a neighboring farmer delivered him safety to their front door. Richard was smiling because he had had the time of his life trying to find his way home.

Eva did something right in raising her children, including Richard, because her name is Eva Branson. Her son, Richard Branson, is one of the richest people in the world and has successfully run many businesses, including Virgin Airlines, Virgin Records, and many other companies.

Here are Eva Branson's five lessons for her kids and life:

1. Live with no regrets.
2. Learn to survive fast.
3. Put others first.
4. Keep your feet on the ground.
5. Every day is a fresh chance.

At the end of her book, *Mum's the Word*, Eva's parting thoughts are timeless. She said,

> When my grandchildren ask me what I've learned the past 80 plus years on earth, I tell them being happy is different for everyone. For me the necessary ingredients for happiness are being open to change, having constructive hobbies, playing one or two sports, keeping an open mind towards others' thoughts and ideas, never seeing too much of one person and always finding time for volunteer work. It is most important to have a lovely family and nothing can replace being with the people you love.
>
> I believe that one door has to close for another one to open. There is no use in wasting time with regret when there is always something constructive to do, including reaching out to others

in need. One must never feel self-pity, as there is always someone who would gladly trade places with you. It is important to see the humor in life and to laugh as often as you can.

Never live in fear—there are always more adventures to follow. There is always another language to learn, another person to meet, another child to encourage, another memorable moment with family and friends, another galaxy to explore. And of course, there's always another book to write. In the meantime, "Mum's the word!"

CHAPTER 26

Be Strong, Stand Up, and Stand Out by Helping Other Women Succeed

There should be a special place in Hell for women
who don't help other women succeed!
—Madeline Albright, former secretary of state

Men do high fives or fist bumps to encourage each other. Women need our own way to celebrate each other's success. We need to stop the misperception that women are backstabbers and are more likely to shoot each other down than help and support one another. We need to work together so we all succeed.

We need to encourage and support each other more than criticize or put each other down. We need to congratulate other women in meetings when they do or say something good. Together, we are unstoppable. We need to think like one team of women working together to help everyone rise up.

Give credit to other women in meetings and in person. We can empower and help each other soar. Sheryl Sandberg started a new campaign in June 2016 called "Together We Can" to dispel the myth that women are backstabbers and bring women together as one team in order to be strong, stand up, and stand out. Remember the saying, "United we stand and divided we fall."

If you go to the Lean In's Facebook page, you'll see a great video with a number of female stars talking about the women who inspired them. The messages in this video are very impactful.

Here is a summary of some of the comments in the video:

Behind every powerful woman is another successful woman.
We are more powerful when we empower each other.
We are more courageous when we encourage others.
We are allies, not rivals.
Together, we are smarter, funnier, bolder, and more powerful.
Together, we'll get to equity.
Together, we raise our voices.
Together, we can stand up to anything and anyone.
When we lean in together, we accomplish amazing things.
Let's lean in together.
And my line…let's go kick some glass!

Find a Mentor and Be a Mentor—Pay It Forward

You can't be an empowered woman unless
you empower other women!
—OPRAH WINFREY

Until recently, one thing men tended to do more than women was find a mentor or be a mentor. I've had a number of mentors in life, both women and men. I used my mentors to give me advice on a career or job choice. My mentors helped me prepare for big presentation, so my message was clear and came across correctly. I used my mentors as a sounding board to bounce different ideas off before I made my decision.

Most of mentorship relationships lasted a few years. We would meet once a month for coffee or lunch. Some of my mentors gave me books or articles to read.

One of my mentors, Sherri, was several management levels higher than I was at the time. She took a special interest in my career and really took me under her wing. She gave me some good leadership books to read, and we would discuss any issues or problems I was having at work.

One day after a big meeting, I started to pick up the empty coffee cups and plates. She gave me a look like I had done something wrong and told me to stop picking up the cups. Sherri pointed out that none of the men bothered to help clean up and neither should the female leaders in the meeting. In her mind, picking up the cups made us look like followers and not leaders. She said, "Everyone has a mother, and you don't need to be their mother and clean up after them."

In most cases, mentors are in a higher-level position than you, and if they work for the same company, they are from a different department. There needs to be considerable trust on both the mentor and the mentee side of the equation. The mentee needs to be able to openly discuss a problem, a challenge, a success, and a potential job change. The mentor needs to be able to give advice and coaching in complete confidentiality.

One of my favorite senior leaders at Microsoft was a man named Orlando Ayala. During my opening interview protocol for my research, I would tell people I would not use their full name in the book without the permission. When I told Orlando this, he said, "If you don't use my full name, then I won't talk to you."

Orlando is an amazing leader, a strategic thinker with the heart to do the right thing and the courage to make a tough call when he needs to do the right thing for the business. Orlando's responses to my questions were inspiring, motivating, and enlightening.

At one point, he talked about how he only mentored women. When I asked why, he said he did not have the time or patience to mentor men because their big egos got in the way. He said the women he mentored were eager to learn, open to feedback, and followed through on making improvements to be a better leader. Men, on the other hand, did not listen as well or usually had a reason and would rationalize why something would not work.

To this day, Orlando is the kind of leader I admire. I often tell people in my seminars and webinars that Orlando is the kind of leader people want to follow. I would walk through hot coals to do something to help Orlando because he is just that kind of leader.

There was a movie out a number of years ago called *Pay It Forward*. The movie is about a little boy who passes positive things on to others and then says, "Pay it forward." I've seen in the newspaper or on the news where someone in the drive-up window pays for the coffee of the person behind him or her and then says, "Pay it forward," so the good deeds continue throughout the day.

If you are in a team leader or senior leader role, part of your job is to "Pay it forward" by being a mentor, especially for younger women. Many companies have formal mentorship programs to help match mentors with mentees. If your company does not have one, find a young woman to help. Provide coaching and advice to help her become a strong and successful female leader. Her future and our future as citizens of the world depend on developing our leaders of the future.

Take Special Care of the Children in Your Life

Build someone up…
Put their insecurities to sleep…
Remind them they are worthy…
Tell them they are incredible…
Be a light in an all too dim world!
—ANONYMOUS

If you are a parent, sister, aunt, or big sister, you need to take time to take special care of the children in your life or the children you meet along the way. Remember the UCLA study that said the average child hears twenty-eight negative comments to every positive comment. I am sure the number is higher today, given things like cyberbullying and some of the things that happen on the school grounds.

I am sure this is controversial, and remember, you don't have to agree with me, but I think we need to teach our children many lessons in life, including sometimes there is a winner in some situations.

There seems to be a trend to give every child a participant ribbon for being part of a team. I think this is fine when kids are very young, but the kid who studies hard to win the National Spelling Bee for being the best speller that year deserves a special award. Kids who practice and work hard to win all of their soccer or any games need to be able to take pride in being a winner.

I think children need to know there are rules to the games they play and they should play by the rules and play well with others. Children also need to know in games and in life, sometimes there are winners and losers. Losing a game does not make you a bad person, but there are many lessons to be learned from losing.

I love a recent commercial where the young boy brings home a participant trophy. The dad grabs the trophy, takes off the participant sign, and writes "CHAMPS" with a Magic Marker.

Be present in the lives of the children around you. Whether you are a mom, dad, sister, brother, aunt, or uncle, take time to help grow great kids. The children of today will one day be running the world.

I feel lucky and blessed to have two wonderful children, Ross III and Elke, who both turned out to be great adults because my husband and I tried our best to raise them in a loving household. We taught them to always do their best and believe they could accomplish anything they put their minds to.

We certainly had our share of ups, downs, and mistakes as well as successes along the way. I remember one time, I came home from work and was busy reading something work related. Ross III came up to me to tell me about his day at school. To be honest, I was half listening, but I nodded my head and said, "Uh-huh."

Ross stood there for a few minutes; he had noticed I was not present or listening to him. He grabbed the papers out of my hand and loudly demanded, "Listen to me." Thanks for the lesson in parenting, Ross III.

I have a special message for dads, brothers, uncles, and the men of the world. I am the person I am today because I had a loving and caring Dad who took time to teach me many things. As I mentioned before, he worked a lot, and many times, he worked the night shift or late-afternoon shift. Yet he always took time to teach me to play tennis, change a tire, and change the oil and the spark plugs on my car. He taught me about sports, playing by my own rules, and being an independent thinker. He attended my school and sporting events and took a genuine interest in me.

Pay it forward!

A Plug for STEM (Science, Technology, Engineering, and Math)

Most of my close friends were probably surprised when I went to work for Microsoft. I worked in banking and ran my own consulting company for ten years, but I had no experience in high tech or information technology.

While my consulting business had done very well for many years, there was something missing in my life. I started to realize while I loved my work and my clients, I missed being able to see a project through all the way to the end and be there to see something I started flourish over and beyond the initial kickoff.

The analogy I use to explain how I left is one many women can relate to—the joy of giving birth. I felt like I had endured the long nine months of pregnancy, including the weight gain, mood swings, and crazy cravings only to give my precious baby up for adoption. I felt empty inside.

I fell in love with Microsoft and how technology really transformed people's lives. I fell in love with the amazingly brilliant and passionate people I worked with at Microsoft. I felt like the company fit my vision and values.

I am not a techie or a "propeller head," which is what many of us in sales and marketing called the engineers and researchers. Due to the number of presentations I needed to build again and again for myself and some of the executives, I got really good at PowerPoint and Word, but I still struggle with things like Excel and pivot tables.

If you have a young girl or woman in your life, encourage her to continue to focus on her natural talent for math and science. If you are a young woman in college or starting your career, get some additional schooling or training in science, technology, and math.

The biggest reason is to build your strengths in these areas, as every job today requires good computer skills. If you want to be a fashion designer, you need to know how to use a computer to design your clothes. If you want to be a teacher, doctor, nurse, marketing professional, or business owner, you need good computer skills. And if you want to change the world, you might want to consider a job with a technology company.

When Steve Jobs was trying to recruit John Scully from PepsiCo to come run Apple, he said, "Do you want to continue to sell sugar water, or do you want to change the world?" John decided to join Apple.

One of my favorite jobs at Microsoft was when I was a "demo dolly." Yes, that is what they used to call the women who demonstrated Microsoft technology to companies and customers. I demonstrated the Microsoft Home of the Future.

Most of the technology you see in the world today, I was demonstrating to customers and partners in the Microsoft Home of the Future in the year 2000. For example, the front door did not have a key, but there was a panel that read my eye and the door would open.

When I walked in the door, I would touch a panel and my favorite music would come on, the lights would come on, and the right windows would open. There was a talking refrigerator. I could ask if we had any Snapple in the house, and the refrigerator would respond, "You have three raspberry tea Snapples left."

Every year, Microsoft would host a special day called, "Take Your Daughters to Work Day." This special day for girls has now evolved to be "Take Your Kids to Work Day" so boys can attend as well.

Part of the day always included a tour of the Microsoft Home, and I always volunteered for this event. I would give the kids a tour of the home and point out all the fun technology. At the end of the tour, I would sit the kids, usually ages seven to sixteen, in the living room area of the home.

I would tell them I used to work with Mattel; the company was one of my clients for five years. I would tell them I worked with the Barbie team, including the team that created the popular designer Bob Mackie Barbie dolls, which sold for over $1,000.

My story included many examples of how cool it was to work at Mattel, but as my son pointed out one day when I came home from an off-site retreat the Barbie senior leadership team went on, "Mom, it's just a doll." My response was, "Yeah, it is just a doll, but Barbie dolls make $2.5 billion a year, which contributes to the US economy."

I ended my story and the demonstration of the home by telling them that if they decided to go into information technology or STEM, they could change people's lives. If you worked in fields like science technology, engineering, and math, you could help a young child who can't see communicate with his or her sighted friends via text messaging. You could be working on a project to cure cancer or help get rid of terrible things like malaria, which kills millions of people in some parts of the world.

Thank goodness for shows like *The Big Bang Theory*, where it is cool to be a geek. Thank goodness for actors like Mayim Bialik, who is not only a talented actress but also a PhD and neuroscientist.

The other reason to consider a career in a STEM field is there is a huge talent shortage of women in this area. Not only is every female college graduate guaranteed a job after graduation, but on average, their starting salary is double their non-STEM peers. There are over five hundred thousand open jobs in IT, and every company is looking for qualified women to join them.

If you are a parent of a young girl, encourage her to continue to utilize her natural talent in science and math. Encourage her to enter science and math contests at school. Make it cool to be smart after the age of ten or eleven. There are wonderful events that encourage kids to put their science and math skills to work, including Advancing Women in Technology's Dream Fest.

Highlight and showcase smart women who use their brains to change the world. I volunteer at a group called Girls Inc., and I've been asked to participate in interview panels or focus groups for the girls of Girls Inc. At one recent event for middle-school girls, they spent a week at Santa Ana Community College, working on different science, math, and technology projects.

On the last day, women like myself, including, a doctor, a woman who owned a construction company, and a woman who worked as a scientist at a large health-care company participated in speed-dating-type small-group discussions.

The three other women and I would sit at one table, and a group of six to eight young girls would come to one of our tables for fifteen minutes. We would spend about five minutes telling the young girls what we did, and then we would open the conversation for questions. At the end of the fifteen minutes, a bell would ring and the girls would move on to the next table.

The one question one of the girls would always ask was "How much do you make?" I would tell them how much I made and how I'd traveled the world on someone else's dime, and their eyes would light up. I closed my short session with the girls by telling them they needed to embrace the idea of going into a STEM career and field if they wanted to change people's lives, travel the world, and make a lot of money.

CHAPTER 27

MY PERSONAL SEVEN THINGS EVERY WOMAN SHOULD DO

There is something about the number seven that is magical. There are the seven summits for people who want to climb the highest mountains in the world. There are the seven wonders of the world. And there are the seven deadly sins.

Here are seven steps to help you jump-start your efforts to be the kind of leader and person you want to be. It is within your power to change. You can be the person you want to be.

1. Love yourself, and put yourself first on your to-do list.
2. Be kind to yourself and others.
3. Do what you love, and the money will follow.
4. Be true to yourself, and never let anyone define you or your self-worth.
5. Stretch, grow, and learn something new every day.
6. Help others succeed, especially young girls and other women.
7. Life is a journey. Enjoy the ride!

This Book Almost Never Got Written

I mentioned it took me three years to research and write this book, but it almost didn't get written or finished. One of the reasons I know some of the techniques in this book is that I applied them to my life when I fell off the top of the corporate ladder, and they worked again about a year and a half later when I stumbled but did not fall.

After I left Microsoft, I spent about six months doing research and working on my book, but then I got stuck. I not only had a bit of writer's block, but I let my own internal negative thoughts and self-talk stop me from achieving this important goal in my life.

I was afraid to write my book and follow my passion and my vision *to make a difference and empower people to be the best they can be.* My thoughts turned to things like, "What if nobody buys my book?" or "What if people don't like it or, even worse, hate it?" Better yet, "Who am I, and why do I have the right to tell people how to be a great female leader?"

I literally stopped writing and doing research. At one point, in our old house, I had different colored three-by-five-inch index cards on the wall with different thoughts or points I wanted to cover in the book. I realized when we moved to a new place recently that I took the cards down, put them away for six months, and stopped writing because of my own self-limiting beliefs.

Finally, on Easter Sunday at church with my sister and her family, a lightning bolt hit me. I felt like someone was saying to me, "Snap out of it!" I came home and found part of my book on my computer and started to write. I have not stopped since that day, and I write every day.

The one interesting thing that happened at the same time is I had a wake-up call for my business. This time, when I stumbled but did not fall, I went back to my vision, my gratitude attitude, and my healthy morning routine. I started to naturally wake up every day at 5:30 a.m., motivated to drive my business forward and finish my first book.

I started attending networking events, and things just started to fall into place naturally. I had energy and passion again. I felt great and had confidence again that I was smart and damn good at what I did. My business was going well, and I was loving what I was doing.

I was on a quest to finish my book in three months, and I did it! July 4, 2016, became my Independence Day, since I wrote the last page and last word on July 4 before heading to a friend's house to watch the fireworks.

One final story before I go. There is a story I love about a famous writer who was sitting on the beach one day, looking for the inspiration to write his next story. He was watching what looked like a dancer. The dancer was running into the sea and throwing something into the water.

Curious, the writer walked closer and realized it was a teenage boy who was throwing starfish back in the ocean. The starfish had beached themselves far from the water and were in danger or dying. The writer walked up to the boy and said, "What are you doing?"

The boy responded, "I am throwing the starfish back in the ocean to save them."

The writer responded, "There are hundreds of starfish on the shore; you can't possibly save all of them."

The young boy ignored the writer, leaned down, and threw another starfish in the water. He said, "It made a difference to that one." The writer started to walk away but came back in the afternoon and spent the rest of the day throwing starfish in the water with the boy.

This book is my starfish to the women of the world who want to be the best leader they can be.

A few final words to consider to help you become the kind of leader you want to be:

Play your game by your own rules.
Don't let anyone define you or your self-worth.
Reach for the stars and always do your best.
Play to your strengths.
Embrace and support people who are different from you.
Let your spirit fly.
Let your voice be heard.
Now…let's go kick some glass!

Final Personal Leadership Action Plan Part 5

1. Review the previous sections of this book, and put into action the one that best fits your current situation.
2. Once you finish the first steps, review the book again and add a few new action steps to help you become the leader you want to be.
3. Just do it.

"The secret of genius
is to carry the spirit of the child into old age,
which means never losing your enthusiasm."
Aldous Huxley

ABOUT THE AUTHOR

Pattie S. Grimm has been recognized for her many successes as a top female leader. She is also an author, speaker, leadership and team development consultant who focuses on empowering others to be the best they can be.

Pattie brings over twenty-five years of senior leadership experience in the primarily male dominated fields of Financial Services and Information Technology. Pattie runs her own organizational effectiveness, team and leadership development firm which helps organization, leaders and teams to achieve their full potential.

Pattie helps businesses, organizations and leaders to lean in to change and uncertainty and lead with a confident sense of boldness and vigor that is required to succeed. She helps people lead their organizations, their careers and themselves with authenticity and purpose.

Pattie is a frequent keynote presenter and speaker on Creating a Customer Centric Culture, High Performance Leadership and Women in Leadership. Pattie is listed as one of the top women business leaders by Worldwide Who's Who for Excellence in Leadership Development.

She lives in Laguna Niguel, California, with her husband of thirty-four years and their pug, Roxie. She has two children and two grandchildren. In her free time, she likes to cook, travel, and relax on the beach with a stack of reading materials.

In addition to *Quiet Women Never Changed History*, she coauthored The Team Development Playbook. Pattie is currently working on several new books including a humorous book on her countless hours and millions of miles of business travel and a book on how to manage the conflict between Millennials and Baby Boomers.

Made in the USA
San Bernardino, CA
11 January 2018